ORACLE QUICK GUIDES
PART 4 - ADMINISTRATION
SECURITY AND PRIVILEDGE

Malcolm Coxall

Edited by Guy Caswell

Cornelio
B
o
o
k
s

Published by M.Coxall - Cornelio Books
Copyright 2016 Malcolm Coxall
First Published in Spain, United Kingdom 2016
ISBN: 978-84-945305-1-7

"Space does not exist unless there are objects in it

Nor does time exist without events."

Contents

Preface and Audience

The subject of security in Oracle is central to the safe use of this enterprise-grade database and the integrity of the data it contains, thus Oracle provides a sophisticated range of methods for managing both data security and user privilege. Consequently this methodology is the subject of this Oracle Quick Guide volume.

As in other databases, the term "security" has several facets. It refers to the limits of the data a user can see and manipulate. However, the term "database security" also refers to the limitation of user actions in what we refer to as their "privileges".

In both cases a "user" may be an end-user of varying rank and privilege working with an application using an Oracle database. However, it may also refer to a software developer, a system administrator, an application support user and indeed even the system owner and their DBA team. All such users have widely varying needs in terms of what data they can and need to see and what privileges they are granted by a database owner.

Oracle Quick Guides: Oracle Quick Guides is a series of quick learning guides for Oracle designers, developers and system managers.

Guide Audience: These guides are designed to rapidly deliver key information about Oracle to the following audience groups:

- Project Managers, Team Leaders and Testers who are new to Oracle and need rapid access to strategic information about the Oracle development environment.

- Business Analysts, Designers and Software Developers who are new to Oracle and need to make a first step in gaining a detailed understanding of the design and development issues involved in Oracle.

- New entrant Oracle DBAs that need a rapid induction in Oracle database administration.

Guide Contents: Oracle Quick Guides have been divided by subject matter. They become increasingly complex and more specific the later the volume. Thus the early volumes are quite general but later volumes are more technical and specific.

Our Objective: There are plenty of Oracle textbooks and user manuals on the market. Most of them are huge and only partly relevant to a particular group of readers. Therefore we decided to divide the subject into smaller, more targeted volumes in order that you only get the information YOU actually need.

For example, a project manager doesn't need to know about some of the more esoteric programming tips, but will need to know some of the strategic issues affecting design and testing. In a similar way, a programmer is much more interested in the syntactic details of a piece of software than in the strategic issues affecting the choice of an Oracle upgrade path.

And so we have targeted these guides at particular groups with specific interests whilst trying to avoid overloading readers with too much detail or extraneous material.

Assumptions: We assume that the reader will be using Oracle 9i, 10g or 11g, although most of the material may apply equally to earlier versions of the Oracle RDBMS.

---oOo---

1. Oracle Database Security Architecture

1.1 Introduction

Oracle provides an extremely secure, flexible and granular system of database security and privilege which is unsurpassed in the world of relational databases.

The central concept in Oracle database security is the Oracle user. Whether you are a DBA, a developer or an end-user, whether you access an Oracle database using command line SQL, or are an application user accessing a backend Oracle database via a public website, you always address an Oracle database as a particular Oracle user.

Oracle users are allocated very specific data, object and system privileges when the user is created and these privileges define the extent of what that Oracle user can see or do within a particular Oracle database.

These aspects of database security are managed in Oracle by associating a user with particular data, object and system privileges by a security administrator or DBA. We will discuss these concepts in more detail in the remainder of this chapter.

Data Security Privileges: The concept of an Oracle user is obviously just a part of the picture of Oracle security. Oracle data security architecture deals with access to the "database objects" which are being secured, i.e. the database tables and their rows of data and how a particular user may create, view or alter this data. Clearly, not all users have the same access to all data and not all users may manipulate data in the same way. For instance, a manager may see or alter almost everything, whereas a customer may see or alter just a fraction of the data relevant to them.

Database Object Privileges: In a similar way, not all users have the same rights over the database itself. A DBA user may be able to create a database object such as a table or index, whereas a developer or ordinary user generally would not have such powerful system privileges.

1.2 Overview of the Oracle Security Architecture

The following are the key concepts used in the Oracle Security Architecture. Here we introduce these concepts and later we will define exactly how they are used.

1.2.1 The DBA: A DBA is a special user created by the system owner. A DBA user (and there may be many) is responsible for all other users of a database, their creation and their privileges. A DBA is also a user, but a user with *super* privileges.

1.2.2 Grant and Revoke: In general, privileges are allocated to users using a "grant" and privileges can be removed from a user using a "revoke".

1.2.3 User: As discussed, the concept of an Oracle user is central to Oracle security. An Oracle user is created by an Oracle DBA user and granted various privileges.

It is often inconvenient or practically impossible to create real Oracle users for every application user. Therefore, in some applications (particularly web-based applications) a single Oracle user may be used to provide access to many "real", external users. This scenario creates its own security problems and solutions.

1.2.4 Privilege: A privilege, in Oracle terms, is divided into two concepts:

- DML privileges
- DDL privileges

The following definitions explain these divisions of privilege:

a/ DML (Object) Privileges: DML privileges provide a user with the rights to see or manipulate certain *data* within a specific database. This generally refers to the privileges to INSERT, UPDATE, DELETE, SELECT data from a particular database TABLE (or view). These rights are referred to as DML command privileges because they refer to the use of "DML" commands meaning "Data Modification Language". These object privileges are generally allocated to each user by a DBA responsible for a particular database's data security based on the needs of the user.

Examples: The following examples show how users are granted DML (INSERT, UPDATE, DELETE, SELECT) privileges to particular tables and how these privileges are revoked:

```
GRANT    SELECT
ON       ORDERS
TO       USER291;

GRANT    INSERT
ON       ORDER_LINES
TO       USER291;

GRANT    UPDATE,
         DELETE
ON       ORDER_LINES
TO       USER292;

REVOKE   INSERT
ON       ORDER_LINES
FROM     USER293;
```

b/ DDL System Privileges: These privileges refer to rights as a database user to carry out certain actions to create, alter or drop certain database objects (such as a table). These and other commands are referred to as DDL commands. DDL refers to a range of powerful SQL syntax known as Data Definition Language, used in the management of database objects.

Obviously, not all users can carry out all tasks in a database. For instance, a DBA responsible for managing a database has very significant privileges, namely to use DDL commands. Generally speaking, a DBA will have the right to CREATE or DROP any database object, or, for example, GRANT or REVOKE other users any privileges he/she chooses.

Clearly, some users such as developers may need the right to CREATE, ALTER or DROP some database objects. In these cases a DBA grants such rights to these development users as required. In a similar way, ordinary functional end-users of different kinds may need some DDL rights in order to execute software addressing the database.

Examples: The following examples show how DDL (System) privileges may be granted or revoked from a user:

```
GRANT     CREATE TABLE,
          CREATE VIEW
TO        USER295;
REVOKE    CREATE VIEW
FROM      USER296;
```

1.2.5 Roles: A role groups together several privileges so that they can be granted to and revoked from one or more users simultaneously. Roles make user privilege management much more convenient. For instance, if a group of users can all SELECT and DELETE from a particular set of tables in exactly the same way, then it makes sense to create a role which includes all these identical privileges and then grant the user to this role. A DBA enables the role for a user before the user can use it. Roles, once defined, can also be grouped into other roles to build a standard matrix of user roles against which any user will fit. This saves a lot of user administration time when a new user is added to a database.

1.2.6 Overview of users, roles and privileges: Here is a simplified diagram in which we can see how users, roles and privileges are related with and without using roles:

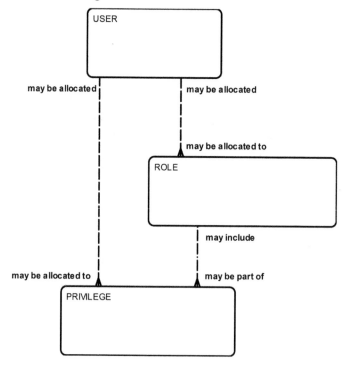

From this diagram it should be clear that a user may be granted privileges directly or may be granted a role, which, in turn, has been granted one or more privileges. A user can also be granted a combination of one or more roles AND separate personal privileges. In fact, any privilege can be granted to many users, and that privilege may be granted to many roles and a role may be allocated to many users. This regime provides a DBA with limitless flexibility and convenience in granting and revoking user privileges.

1.2.7 Profiles: One aspect of Oracle database security relates to the resource usage allocated to a user and to how their password and login is managed. This is often controlled using a "profile". Profiles are created by DBAs to control password validity, duration, and the number of allowed failed logins, for instance. Profiles can also be used to control CPU usage limits, connect time limits, idle time limits, logical reads per call and per session etc.

Clearly, one aspect of Oracle security must deal with the potential of a user attempting to log in many times. Thus profiles help to protect against the eventuality of an unauthorised login attempt by limiting the number of failed login attempts.

Similarly, a DBA must defend the database against extreme CPU usage by one or more users which could have severe effects on database performance and other users. Again a profile allows limits to be set which can reduce this risk. Examples: The following example sets a limit on the number of times a password may be reused:

```
CREATE PROFILE   new_profile
LIMIT            PASSWORD_REUSE_MAX   8
                 PASSWORD_REUSE_TIME  40;
```

The following profile definition limits resource usage:

```
CREATE  PROFILE                        app_user
        LIMIT
        SESSIONS_PER_USER              UNLIMITED
        CPU_PER_SESSION                UNLIMITED
        CPU_PER_CALL                   3000
        CONNECT_TIME                   45
        LOGICAL_READS_PER_SESSION      DEFAULT
        LOGICAL_READS_PER_CALL         1000
        PRIVATE_SGA                    15K
        COMPOSITE_LIMIT                5000000
```

1.3 User and Privileges in the Data Dictionary

Clearly, with many users, roles and privileges, the matrix of users and roles in a large organisation using Oracle-based systems can quickly become extremely unwieldy and complex. For this reason it is essential for the DBA to be able to see all defined users and privileges as they are currently defined. This may be done by querying certain Oracle Data Dictionary tables. This is discussed in more detail in Chapter 12.

1.4 The Least Privilege Principle

An important principle in database security (including in an Oracle environment) is the concept referred to as the "Least Privilege Principle". This principle basically states that "all users should be granted the absolute minimum of privileges necessary to fulfil their tasks".

A DBA or security administrator should always follow the principle of "least privilege" when granting privileges to users. This entails a policy of granting no more privileges to any user than those that are *essential* to them for carrying out their basic functions.

---o0o---

2. Managing Oracle User Security

Every Oracle database has a number of valid database users. In order to access an Oracle database a user must be executing some form of database application using a valid user id and password. This Oracle user id is normally created by the database administrator (DBA).

There are a number of ways in which user ids are created and limited in an Oracle database. These include setting limits on what a user can do or see and limiting the system resources that a database user can employ. Oracle's internal data dictionary provides many ways to query the definition of users and the resources and sessions that they use.

- "Profiles" provide a convenient way for a DBA to set up a range of common user resource and login limits which can be applied to many users.

- "Roles" provide a way to define a group of object and system privileges which can also be applied to many users.

Profiles and roles are thus very important aspects in day to day user management for the DBA.

2.1 Creating a New User Account

When a new user account is required a DBA is normally responsible for the account creation. A DBA is a user, normally granted the privilege to create other new users.

The basic command to create a user uses the following syntax:

```
CREATE USER      <username>
IDENTIFIED BY    <password>;
```

2.1.1 User Naming Conventions: *<username>* is any valid user id and the *<password>* is a user password to allow for the user account creation. A password can be up to 30 characters in length.

Generally speaking, a DBA will use a standard user-naming convention which makes it easy to remember consistent user names and avoid the risk of duplication. Very often they will use the first initial and last name of a user followed by a number (without spaces), for instance psmith01 for Paul Smith. The number allows for 99 other Paul Smiths. An alternative system uses the activity of the user as a standard user name. For instance, a person entering invoices to an accounting system may be referred to as an invoice entry clerk. A username could be designed to reflect this role and in this case a valid username might be "invoice_entry01". The benefit of using fixed user ids for a particular activity is that users can be created at the time a system is commissioned and these user ids can be re-used if employees change. The disadvantage of using pre-defined user ids is that any auditing functionality in an application will only identify the generic user id and does not easily identify a single individual.

2.1.2 Defining Users and Resources they can use: The basic CREATE USER syntax is rarely used alone because such a user would have no privileges and indeed would be unable to connect to a database. In practice, a DBA will create a user and allocate them a DEFAULT TABLESPACE and a TEMP TABLESPACE as well as sometimes setting quotas on their use of these and other tablespaces in the database. The DBA may also allocate the user to a particular profile which has already been defined by the DBA. This profile will define login and resource usage limits to be applied to this and other users. Finally, the DBA will grant the CREATE SESSION privilege to the user in order that they can connect to the database. The following example illustrates a typical user creation script:

```
CREATE USER              invoice_entry01
IDENTIFIED BY            <password>
DEFAULT TABLESPACE       invoices_ts
QUOTA                    300M
ON                       training_ts
QUOTA                    100K
ON                       invoices_ts
TEMPORARY TABLESPACE     temp_01
PROFILE                  accounts_clerk;

GRANT CREATE SESSION TO   invoice_entry01;
```

2.1.3 Allocating Tablespaces and Quotas to a User: From an administrative and performance point of view it is important that database objects are created within an appropriate tablespace. This can be defined when creating a user account.

2.1.3.1 User Tablespaces: In an Oracle database the default tablespace (where database objects are created) is the SYSTEM tablespace. If a user does not create database objects such as tables, and has no privileges to do so, then this default setting is fine. However, if a user, such as a developer, is likely to create any type of object, then the DBA

14

should assign the user a default tablespace, such as the USERS tablespace or some new tablespace for the creation of a developer's own objects. If no user default tablespace is specified when creating a user then the user will, by default, use the SYSTEM tablespace.

This use of the SYSTEM tablespace for user objects should be avoided. The reason for this is that if a user uses the SYSTEM tablespace for their database objects this may cause unnecessary contention between data dictionary objects allocated to the SYSTEM tablespace and those objects created by the user in the SYSTEM tablespace. This is because both types of objects are stored in the same physical data files. Contention for user objects that are created in the SYSTEM tablespace can have profoundly negative effects on database performance. So the rule is that, in general, user objects and data must never be stored in the SYSTEM tablespace. Thus it is very important to specify the user's default tablespace when creating a user account according to their particular needs, especially if they create tables or other database objects.

Note: A separate *default* permanent tablespace can also be created after the database is created and this provides an alternative to specifying every user's default tablespace. This default tablespace is not used by SYSTEM or SYS, nor does it contain data dictionary objects and therefore contention is avoided.

2.1.3.2 Quotas on Tablespaces: In order for a user such as a developer to be able to create objects in a tablespace, they should be allocated a space quota on their default tablespace. A DBA can also assign each user a tablespace quota for any tablespace (except a temporary tablespace).

By default, a user has no quota on any tablespace in the database. Quotas are important, particularly for users that need to create database objects such as tables. If the user has the privilege to create a schema object, then the DBA must assign a quota to allow the user to create objects. As a minimum, a DBA must assign users a quota for their default tablespace.

Whilst allocating tablespace quotas is most relevant to developers, some database applications also allow users to create database objects such as temporary tables; therefore the allocation of quotas may be applicable to normal functional users as well as to developers.

Quotas limit the amount of space that is allocated for storage of user database objects within the specified tablespace. Quotas prevent a user's objects from using too much space in the database. Quotas can be allocated when a user account is created (as in the last example) or can be allocated later using the ALTER USER syntax:

```
ALTER USER    <username>
QUOTA         100M
ON            tablespace_name;
```

An option also exists to grant a user an unlimited quota on all tablespaces. This can be useful but is rather unselective. The UNLIMITED TABLESPACE grant effectively overrides any quotas for a user. UNLIMITED TABLESPACE is a privilege granted by the DBA as follows:

```
GRANT   UNLIMITED TABLESPACE
TO      <username>;
```

A DBA can revoke a user's ability to use a particular tablespace by using the ALTER USER syntax and setting their quotas to zero. This effectively stops a user from creating any new objects in the specified tablespace - the user's existing objects are unaffected however.

A DBA can find a definition of all existing user quotas by querying the USER_TS_QUOTAS view.

2.1.3.3 Temporary Tablespace: A temporary tablespace is used by Oracle when it is necessary to perform large sorting or join operations which exceed the available RAM of a server. In such an event the temporary tablespace acts as temporary storage to allow the sorting or join operation to be completed.

The DBA should assign a temporary tablespace to each user in the database to prevent them from allocating sort space in the SYSTEM tablespace. This is also important to minimise contention for the SYSTEM tablespace. The assignment of a temporary tablespace to a user can be done either when the user is created using CREATE USER syntax as stated above or can also be done after a user is created using the ALTER USER syntax:

```
CREATE USER             <username>
DEFAULT TABLESPACE      data_ts
TEMPORARY TABLESPACE    temp;
```

This syntax creates a user with the default tablespace data_ts and their temporary tablespace called temp. Obviously both tablespaces must exist before they are allocated to a user. The statement below alters an existing user and allocates the temporary tablespace called temp to that user:

        ALTER USER   <username>
        TEMPORARY TABLESPACE   temp;

Note: Remember that if your SYSTEM tablespace is locally managed, then users must be assigned a specific default (locally managed) temporary tablespace. They may not be allowed to default to using the SYSTEM tablespace because temporary objects cannot be placed in locally managed permanent tablespaces.

2.1.4 Assigning a Profile to a User: A profile (as we shall see in the next chapter) defines a set of limits on database resources and password-protected access to the database. Profiles are created by the DBA and users may be defined with a particular profile that is appropriate to their functional requirements.

If a user is created without specifying a profile, then the Oracle Database assigns the user a default profile. The syntax to assign a user to a profile is part of the CREATE USER syntax (see example above). An existing user can be assigned to a profile using the ALTER USER syntax. In both cases the profile being assigned must already be defined by the DBA:

        ALTER USER   <username>
        PROFILE   profile_name;

2.1.5 Setting a Default Role for the User: A role is a group of privileges that a DBA grants to one or more users or to other roles. A user can be granted many roles but sometimes it is useful to choose just one of the granted roles as the default role. This default role is then automatically enabled for a user when the user creates a session (logs into the database). Thus, if a user is granted several roles and one of them is set as the default role, then the other granted roles are ignored. Furthermore, if several roles are assigned to a user, any one or more of these assigned roles may be set as default roles. So if a user has, for instance, 5 roles granted to him, then a DBA may choose to make 3 of these roles default roles.

Default roles cannot be set using the CREATE USER syntax. Default roles can only be set using the ALTER USER syntax as in the following example:

This creates a new role called test_user_role:

```
CREATE ROLE        test_user_role;
```

This syntax grants the privilege SELECT ON ANY TABLE to the new role test_user_role:

```
GRANT   SELECT
ON      ANY TABLE
TO      test_user_role;
```

This statement grants the role to a user called <username>. Obviously a user must have been granted the role before it can be set as the default:

```
GRANT   test_user_role
TO      <username>;
```

The following statement makes this role the only default role for this user. Thereafter, any other roles will be ignored:

```
ALTER               <username>
DEFAULT ROLE   test_user_role;
```

2.2 Altering User Accounts

It is quite common for users to require changes in their accounts after they are created. They may need new or different privileges or they may lose certain privileges because they take on new or different functions or tasks with one or more software applications.

This situation is managed by the DBA group by means of the ALTER USER syntax. Apart from a user being able to change their own passwords, the only users that can alter a user's account are those which have the ALTER USER privilege. This is generally a DBA or other database security personnel.

2.2.1 The ALTER USER syntax: The following example shows how the ALTER USER syntax is phrased:

```
ALTER USER                  <username>
DEFAULT TABLESPACE          data_ts
TEMPORARY TABLESPACE   temp_ts
QUOTA 100M ON               data_ts
QUOTA 0 ON                  test_ts
PROFILE                     clerk;
```

This example of the ALTER USER statement changes the security settings for the user as follows:

18

- The default and temporary tablespaces are explicitly set for the user.

- The user is given a 100M quota for the tablespace data_ts.

- The quota on the tablespace called test_ts is revoked for the user (i.e. set to 0).

- The user is assigned the profile called clerk.

2.2.2 Changing User Passwords: A DBA (or anyone with the ALTER USER privileges) can change any user password as follows:

ALTER USER   <username>
IDENTIFIED BY   <new_password>;

However in order that a user can manage their own password, Oracle provides a method which any user can use to alter their own password if they have access to SQL*Plus. This uses the PASSWORD command:

SQL>PASSWORD <username>
>Changing password for <username>
>New password: <new_password>
>Retype new password: <new_password>

2.2.3 Changing the SYS User Password: The SYS user password may occasionally need to be changed. Because SYS is used by many internal database processes the DBA should be careful when using the ALTER USER syntax to change the SYS password because this may lead to processes becoming deadlocked. If possible choose a time when the database is idle.

A safer alternative is to create a password file using the Oracle command line syntax orapwd as follows (This example is for Unix but works identically in MS versions):

$ orapwd file='orapworcl'

$ Enter password for SYS: <new_password>

---o0o---

3. Managing Privileges and Roles

Privileges can be assigned to users individually but the task of assigning privileges in this way becomes very onerous when there are many users with many different privileges. Maintaining individual privileges becomes almost impossible in even small organisations with several database applications. In small production or development systems this may be tolerable but in larger or more complex production environments assigning individual users with specific privileges is not practical. For this reason, Oracle provides a method by which groups of similar users can be assigned a set of pre-defined privileges. These sets of privileges are referred to as roles.

3.1 Introduction

In general, user privileges are granted to users by a database administrator (DBA). A DBA is given the right to grant user privileges after a database is created by the SYS or SYSTEM user. The SYS and SYSTEM users are automatically created when a database is installed and hold the supreme privileges of the database. A DBA user may connect to a database as SYS or SYSTEM when certain administrative tasks are required though generally a DBA will connect to the database as a normal named user with specific DBA privileges.

The main DBA task of authorising privileges for others includes two main categories of privilege:

- Permitting only certain users to access, process, or alter certain data.

- Applying various limitations on a user's access or actions. The limitations assigned to users apply to objects such as schemas, tables, and database rows and it may also apply to database resources such as database resource time (CPU, connect, or idle time).

Thus a user privilege may give the right to run a particular type of SQL statement, or the right to access an object, such as a table, that belongs to another user or execute a PL/SQL package, etc. The types of privileges are defined within the Oracle Database.

Roles are created by DBAs in order to group together certain privileges (or even other roles). Roles provide a convenient way to facilitate the granting of multiple privileges or roles to users. A user must obviously exist before a role is granted to him. A role must be granted to a user before the user can make use of the role privileges.

3.2 Who should be Granted Privileges?

All database users require some privileges in order to access a database. The types of privileges granted to a user depends entirely upon the tasks that they are required to complete.

A very basic user that needs to query a particular database table needs to be granted CREATE SESSION in order to connect to the database but also needs SELECT privilege on the table(s) that they need to query. A more advanced user may be able to add, delete or update some data and they would need SELECT, INSERT, UPDATE and DELETE privileges on the tables that they are permitted to work on. Developer users may need privileges to create and change their own database objects such as tables and in this case, they would need the system privileges CREATE TABLE and ALTER TABLE. A DBA requires very extensive privileges and may well be granted the SYSDBA or SYSOPER privileges, which we will explain later in this guide.

In general, a DBA grants privileges only to a user that explicitly requires those privileges to accomplish their work. Granting unnecessary privileges compromises security.

A user can receive a privilege in two ways:

- A DBA may grant privileges to users explicitly. For example, a DBA may grant a user the privilege to INSERT records into the INVOICE_LINES table:

> GRANT INSERT ON INVOICE_LINES to <username>;

- As discussed above, a DBA can also grant privileges to a role, and then grant the role to one or more users. For instance, the DBA may create a role INVOICE_CLERK_ROLE and grant SELECT, INSERT, UPDATE and DELETE privileges to that role and then grant the role to one or more users. Generally speaking, privileges should always be granted using roles rather than to users explicitly.

3.2.1 The PUBLIC Role: A special role exists in Oracle called PUBLIC. The PUBLIC role is a special role that every database user account automatically has when the account is created. By default, it has no privileges granted to it. This role can be granted privileges in the same way as any normal role. However, PUBLIC is special because it includes all database users and therefore granting a privilege to PUBLIC needs to be done only after very careful consideration regarding the actual needs of present and future users. Generally speaking, each database user should have only the privileges required to accomplish their current tasks successfully and for this reason the PUBLIC role is rarely used in production databases, though it can be useful in a development environment where users are trusted and where risks to data are limited.

The PUBLIC role cannot be dropped, and a manual grant or revoke of this role has no meaning because the user account always assumes this role. Because all database user accounts assume the PUBLIC role it does not appear in the DBA_ROLES and SESSION_ROLES data dictionary views.

3.3 Categories of Privilege

As already mentioned, there are several categories of privilege:

- Object privileges: These are also sometimes referred to as DML privileges. These privileges provide users with the right to SELECT, INSERT, UPDATE and DELETE certain data in certain tables. These privileges are used to allow normal production users to carry out their work.

- System privileges: Also referred to as DDL privileges. These are powerful privileges that allow users to carry out various actions on schema objects in the database such as CREATE or ALTER TABLE. These privileges are confined to trusted users such as DBAs and developers.

3.3.1 Object Privileges: An object privilege is a right granted by a DBA to a user or role on a database object that the user does not own. Some examples of object privileges include the right to insert data into a particular table, select data from another user's table or execute a stored procedure owned by another user. An object privilege grants permission to perform a particular action on a specific schema object.

The generic syntax for granting and revoking object privileges is as follows:

> GRANT privileges ON object TO user;

> REVOKE privileges ON object FROM user;

Each type of object has different privileges associated with it. A table has privileges to INSERT, UPDATE, DELETE and SELECT for instance, whereas a database procedure has the privilege to EXECUTE associated with it. Some schema objects, such as triggers, clusters, indexes and database links do not have associated object privileges.

Their use is controlled with system privileges. For example, to alter a cluster, a user must own the cluster or have the ALTER ANY CLUSTER system privilege. These system privileges are discussed later.

Object privileges are given and taken away from a user using the GRANT and REVOKE syntax. It is also possible to grant and revoke ALL available object privileges on a database object:

```
GRANT    ALL
ON       INVOICE_LINES
TO       <username>;
```

Apart from the GRANT and REVOKE syntax in SQL*Plus, privileges can also be managed using Oracle Enterprise Manager and various third party tools such as TOAD. The following examples show how the GRANT and REVOKE syntax is used in SQL*Plus:

```
GRANT    SELECT,
         INSERT,
         DELETE,
         UPDATE
ON       INVOICE_LINES
TO       <username>;
REVOKE   DELETE
ON       INVOICE_LINES
FROM     <username>;
```

3.3.1.1 Who Can Grant Schema Object Privileges? A user that owns a schema object has all object privileges for all objects in their schema and can grant any object privilege on any schema object he or she owns to any other user or role.

Also, if a user has the GRANT ANY OBJECT PRIVILEGE they may also grant and revoke any specified object privilege to and from any user to any other user or role. They may even revoke privileges granted by the object owner to other users.

For instance, if user_1 has a table called table_1 and user_2 has the GRANT ANY OBJECT PRIVILEGE, then user_2 can grant or revoke any table privilege to user_3 as in the following example:

```
SQL>connect user_2/password

SQL>grant select on user_1.table_1 to user_3
```

23

3.3.1.2 The WITH GRANT privilege: The WITH GRANT option allows a user to give another user the privilege to pass on a particular privilege to other users. Only the schema user that owns the object can grant privileges to that object unless the WITH GRANT option is included in the syntax. Here is an example of the use of the WITH GRANT option:

GRANT   SELECT,
                            INSERT,
                            DELETE,
                            UPDATE
ON   INVOICE_LINES
TO   <username>
WITH GRANT OPTION;

The WITH GRANT option should be used very carefully because it relinquishes control of object privileges from a central schema owner to other users who can then pass on these privileges to others. Also, when this option is used the original grantor may REVOKE a grant from the original grantee and this causes a cascading effect of loss of privilege to any users already given by the grantee. This cascading effect can have some unpredictable consequences. This option is only available to object privileges. You cannot assign a privilege that includes the WITH GRANT OPTION to a role because this would create an unacceptable security issue.

3.3.1.3 Object Privileges and Synonyms: Synonyms can be created for many Oracle database objects such as tables and views. Privileges can be granted using these synonyms in the same way as if they were being granted on the underlying object and indeed the grant is simply translated into a grant on the underlying object. This needs to be kept in mind when querying the data dictionary looking for granted privileges.

3.3.1.4 Administering Table Privileges: Table privileges allow for the security of DML (data manipulation language) operations such as INSERT and UPDATE and also allow for the security of DDL (data definition language) operations such as ALTER TABLE.

DML Operations: An administrator can grant the following privileges on one or more tables or views: INSERT, UPDATE, DELETE and SELECT to either users or roles. For instance a role ACCOUNTS_CLERK could be granted SELECT on a specific table INVOICE_HEADERS as follows:

```
GRANT    SELECT
ON       INVOICE_HEADERS
TO       ACCOUNTS_CLERK;
```

This has the effect of allowing all users that are part of the ACCOUNTS_CLERK role the ability to query the INVOICE_HEADERS table.

In addition, a DBA can further restrict INSERT and UPDATE operations to certain columns only. This has the effect of allowing a user or role only to INSERT or UPDATE records but only for the specified columns. This is useful if a user or role is only permitted to see or alter certain parts of a record and where other columns may contain confidential data. It is important to note that when granting an INSERT privilege at column level, all the columns that are defined as NOT NULL must be included, otherwise it will not be possible to insert the record and an error will be raised. The following example shows how column level privileges are granted:

```
GRANT    UPDATE (UNIT_PRICE)
ON       INVOICE_LINES
TO       ACCOUNTS_CLERK;
```

In this example the role ACCOUNTS_CLERK is granted the right to update only the UNIT_PRICE column of the INVOICE_LINES table.

A similar restriction can also be achieved by creating a restrictive VIEW using only the columns that the role can UPDATE.

DDL Operations: A DBA can grant the following DDL privileges on a table: REFERENCES, ALTER, INDEX.

REFERENCES Privilege: The REFERENCES privilege allows the granted user to use a column on a table as a parent key for a foreign key in a table owned by that user. Obviously, the parent columns which can be referenced must be part of the primary key or another unique key of the parent table. This privilege then creates a dependency on the parent table and will affect what DML actions are possible on the parent table. Deleting a parent record which is referenced by another table may become impossible without first deleting the "child" records in the referencing table. Therefore care should be taken in granting this privilege. This privilege cannot be granted to a role, only to an individual user.

For instance, to grant a user called ACCOUNTS_DEVELOPER the REFERENCES privilege on the ORDER_HEADERS table, column ORDER_ID the following syntax is used:

```
GRANT    REFERENCES (ORDER_ID)
ON       ORDER_HEADERS
TO       ACCOUNTS_DEVELOPER;
```

This allows the user ACCOUNTS_DEVELOPER to define referential integrity constraints that refer to the ORDER_ID column of the ORDER_HEADERS table. This means that the user could, for example, create their own table referencing the ORDER_ID column in the granted table. For instance, they could create a new table as follows:

```
CREATE TABLE        ORDER_PROGRESS
(PROGRESS_ID        NUMBER,
PROGRESS_STATUS     VARCHAR2(20),
ORDER_REF           NUMBER
CONSTRAINT          IN_ORDERS
REFERENCES          ORDER_HEADERS (ORDER_ID));
```

The constraint IN_ORDERS ensures that the value ORDER_REF in the new table ORDER_PROGRESS corresponds to an ORDER_ID in the ORDER_HEADERS table.

This privilege can be useful during development where developers may need to build new tables with constraints against existing tables.

ALTER Privilege: The ALTER privilege allows a user to change a table's definition using the ALTER TABLE syntax.

The syntax to grant a user the right to alter a table in another schema is as follows:

```
GRANT    ALTER
ON       A.ORDER_HEADERS
TO       <username>;
```

Here an administrator or schema owner of schema A grants the privilege to <username> to ALTER a table in schema A called ORDER_HEADERS. The grantee can then alter the structure of ORDER_HEADERS, adding or modifying columns, adding constraints, etc.

Clearly, allowing a user to alter a table's structure and definition has profound ramifications, so this privilege must be granted sparingly.

INDEX Privilege: The INDEX privilege allows a user to create an INDEX on a table that they do not own. It cannot be granted to a role but only to a user.

```
GRANT   INDEX
ON      A.ORDER_HEADERS
TO      <username>;
```

This grants the user <username> the right to create an index on the table ORDER_HEADERS owned by schema A.

Associated privileges necessary: A user attempting to perform a DDL operation on a table may need additional system or object privileges. For example, to create an index on a table, the user requires both the INDEX object privilege for the table and the CREATE TRIGGER system privilege. The same is true of the ALTER privilege and the REFERENCES privilege.

3.3.1.5 Administering View Privileges: A view is really just a representation of a SQL query that is stored in memory so that it can easily be re-used. For example, if we have a frequently used query, it may be convenient to create a view based on this query. For instance ,we have a common query as follows:

```
SELECT  ORDER_ID
FROM    A.ORDER_HEADERS
WHERE   ORDER_STATUS = 'COMPLETED';
```

We could create a view of this statement for convenience as follows:

```
CREATE VIEW   COMPLETED_ORDERS
AS
SELECT        ORDER_ID
FROM          A.ORDER_HEADERS
WHERE         ORDER_STATUS = 'COMPLETED';
```

This creates a new view called COMPLETED_ORDERS which contains only those ORDER_HEADER records with ORDER_STATUS equal to "COMPLETED". No new data is stored in the database except a data dictionary definition of the VIEW and its underlying query. When the view is queried Oracle actually executes the underlying query against the real base tables defined in the view.

For example, querying the view

```
SELECT   *
FROM     COMPLETED_ORDERS
WHERE    ORDER_ID > 2000;
```

Oracle transforms this query into:

```
SELECT   ORDER_ID
FROM     A.ORDER_HEADERS
WHERE    ORDER_STATUS = 'COMPLETED';
AND      ORDER_ID > 2000;
```

With the appropriate privileges a view can be queried and data can be updated or deleted, and new data inserted directly to a view. These operations directly alter the tables on which the view is based and are subject to the integrity constraints and triggers of the base tables.

You can apply DML object privileges to views in a similar way to tables. Object privileges for a view allow various DML operations which, as noted, affect the base tables from which the view is derived. The object privileges available for views are INSERT, UPDATE, DELETE, SELECT and REFERENCES. The syntax to grant and revoke these privileges is the same as for privileges granted on a table.

Views can be created using tables or other views within a query.

Privileges Required to Create Views: In order to create a view a user must have the necessary system privileges (CREATE VIEW or CREATE ANY VIEW). In addition, the user must have the following object privileges on all the underlying tables or other views: SELECT, INSERT, UPDATE and DELETE.

To grant access to a view based on tables or views in another schema, the object privileges need to have been granted using the WITH GRANT OPTION so that the creator of the view has the right to pass on access to the underlying objects to other users. Not having these privileges will raise an error when an attempt is made to grant access to the view.

View Security - Inherited Privilege: As we have seen, the creator of a view must have access to the underlying tables used in the view they create. When access to the view is granted to someone else, it is the privileges of the view's creator which determine if the view can be used by other users. Thus if the view creator loses the privilege on the underlying tables that are used in the view, then immediately the view becomes unusable for everyone, regardless of whether they have been granted access to the view.

View Security - Value-based Security: A view can provide a powerful means of filtering data so that only certain records are available to certain users by means of a view. For instance, we may want to restrict access to orders of value greater than 5000. We could do that with a view:

```
CREATE VIEW    SMALL_ORDERS
AS
SELECT         *
FROM           A.ORDER_HEADERS
WHERE          ORDER_VALUE <= 5000;
```

View Security - Column-level Security: Views are also useful in determining which data in a record can be seen by certain users. For instance, we might wish to hide certain data from certain users, such as order value. We could do this as follows:

```
CREATE VIEW    NON_FINANCE_ORDERS
AS
SELECT         ORDER_ID, ORDER_DATE,
FROM           A.ORDER_HEADERS;
```

This view would contain all records but only non-financial data. A hybrid of value-based security and column-level security in a view's design can provide very sophisticated and safe data filters for specific user groups.

View security - User-level Security: Views can take advantage of pseudo columns like USER to enforce a data filter. The pseudo column USER returns the currently logged in Oracle userid. So for instance we could filter records according to the id of the records creator if this is stored in the record, as in the following example:

```
CREATE VIEW    MY_ORDERS
AS
SELECT         *
FROM           A.ORDER_HEADERS
WHERE          ORDER_CREATED_BY = USER;
```

3.3.1.6 Administering Sequence Privileges: Sequences allow sequential numbers to be generated without the need to create software to generate them or control their generation. A simple statement such as the following will generate a new sequence automatically, where MY_SEQUENCE is a sequence created in the current schema:

```
SELECT   MY_SEQUENCE.NEXTVAL
FROM     DUAL;
```

A sequence can be used by many users simultaneously and therefore other users and roles must be granted access to each sequence that they will be using. To do this it is necessary to grant SELECT on the sequence as follows:

```
GRANT   SELECT
ON      SCHEMA.MY_SEQUENCE
TO      <username or rolename>;
```

3.3.1.7 Managing Access to Database Procedures and Functions:
As with other objects, database objects, procedures, packages and functions are created within a single schema and their use must be explicitly granted to other users and roles. The only object privilege that can be granted on a procedure to a user or role is the EXECUTE privilege which allows the grantee to execute the procedure or function. This privilege is also required if the grantee wishes to create and compile their own procedure which then calls a procedure in another schema. The syntax to grant this privilege is as follows:

```
GRANT   EXECUTE
ON      SCHEMA.MY_PROCEDURE
TO      <username or rolename>;
```

A user or role can also be granted EXECUTE rights on an entire package or simply on one or more procedures within a package. A list of procedures (separated by commas) can also be granted using the same syntax.

3.3.2 System Privileges:
A system privilege is the right to perform a particular action on any schema object of a particular type. They include many DDL (data definition privileges), and system privileges are therefore extremely powerful and rarely granted to ordinary users.

For example, the privileges to create or alter a table and to update data in *any* table in a database are system privileges. System privileges are normally only granted to DBAs, system administrators and trusted developers and they are only granted when absolutely necessary. Over 100 system privileges are available in Oracle.

Generally speaking, system privileges are confined to those engaged in system management or the development of a database or application software.

Appendix 1 contains a list of common system privileges.

3.3.2.1 Granting and Revoking System Privileges: A DBA can grant or revoke system privileges to users and roles using the GRANT and REVOKE syntax or using the Oracle Enterprise Manager interface.

Only two types of users can grant or revoke system privileges to other users:

- Users who were granted a specific system privilege with the ADMIN OPTION.

- Users with the system privilege GRANT ANY PRIVILEGE (generally a DBA).

The general syntax for granting a system privilege is as follows:

        GRANT   <system privilege>
        TO   <username or rolename>;

The general syntax for revoking a system privilege is as follows:

        REVOKE   <system privilege>
        FROM   <username or rolename>;

3.3.2.2 The ANY Privilege Syntax: A DBA can grant a user or role a system privilege using the ANY syntax. The ANY keyword enables a DBA to set privileges for an entire category of objects in the database. For example, the user here is granted the privilege to ALTER ANY TABLE.

        GRANT   ALTER ANY TABLE
        TO   <username>;

This grants the user the right to alter any table in any database schema. Clearly, this is a very powerful privilege that should only be granted to very trusted administrative personnel. In particular, DBAs should be extremely careful using the ANY keyword when granting privileges to the PUBLIC role.

3.3.2.3 Data Dictionary Security: In certain circumstances it is possible for objects in the data dictionary (owned by SYS) to be maliciously attacked and in particular by users granted privileges with the ANY keyword.

Because the ANY privilege keyword also applies to the data dictionary, a malicious user with ANY privilege could access or alter data dictionary tables with potentially catastrophic results. However, this vulnerability can be avoided by taking the following precautions:

- Set the O7_DICTIONARY_ACCESSIBILITY initialization parameter to FALSE (the default value). A DBA can set this parameter by using an ALTER SYSTEM statement or by modifying the initSID.ora file. This feature is called the dictionary protection mechanism. When the O7_DICTIONARY_ACCESSIBILITY parameter is set to FALSE, system privileges that enable access to objects in any schema (for example, users who have ANY privileges, such as ALTER ANY TABLE) do **NOT** allow access to objects in the SYS schema.

This means that access to the objects in the SYS schema (data dictionary objects) is restricted to users who connect using the SYSDBA privilege. In this case, system privileges that provide access to objects in other schemas do not give other users access to objects in the SYS schema. For example, the SELECT ANY TABLE privilege allows users to retrieve data from tables and views in other schemas, but does not enable them to select from data dictionary tables. A DBA can, however, grant these users explicit object privileges to access objects in the SYS schema using the SELECT ANY DICTIONARY privilege to selected users that need view access to the data dictionary.

- Use the ANY clause of a system privilege **very** sparingly. Only the most trusted system administrators, DBAs and developers should be granted system privileges with the ANY clause.

3.3.2.4 The "WITH ADMIN OPTION" Clause: When granting a system privilege, it is possible to use the WITH ADMIN OPTION clause. Sometimes a DBA may wish to grant privileges to users and enable these users to grant those privileges to other users. This may be the case when a new DBA is added to a team. When this is the case, the grantor may include the WITH ADMIN OPTION keyword in the GRANT command.

When this keyword is used, it will allow the user granted the privilege to grant that privilege to other users. Privileges that are granted WITH ADMIN OPTION can be passed to other users. In some Oracle environments this is considered to be too great a security risk and the use of WITH ADMIN OPTION is often forbidden.

Here is the generic syntax:

```
GRANT                    <system privilege>
TO                       <username>
WITH ADMIN OPTION;
```

It should be noted that when system privileges are passed to others using the WITH ADMIN OPTION, then revoking the system privileges from the original user will **not** cascade to other users. The system privileges granted to others must be revoked directly.

3.4 Granting Privileges to Users and Roles: It is possible for a privileged DBA to allocate privileges to any legitimate Oracle user one privilege at a time, and one user at a time. However, this method of managing privileges soon becomes a very onerous administrative task. Generally speaking, DBAs prefer to manage user privilege using a set of pre-defined roles containing a number of privileges that can then be granted to a user. This is true both for object privileges and for system privileges.

The generic syntax to create a new role is as follows:

```
CREATE ROLE    <rolename>;
```

Once a role is created, then privileges can be granted to the role in the same way that they are granted to a user. The generic syntax for this is as follows:

```
GRANT    <system or object privilege clause>
TO       <rolename>;
```

Finally the role can be granted to a chosen user:

```
GRANT    <rolename>
TO       <username>;
```

3.4.1 Standard Roles - When not to use them: In early releases of Oracle during database creation the installer automatically created 3 standard roles: CONNECT, RESOURCE and DBA. The original basis for these 3 standard roles is that normal application users would be granted the CONNECT role, developers would be granted the RESOURCE role and a systems DBA would be granted the DBA role.

These standard roles still exist for backward compatibility but Oracle recommends that they should not be used and that a System owner and DBA should design their own specific roles for various groups of users. However, these standard roles may still have a place in a controlled development environment but they should never be used in a production environment. This is because they give users more privileges than they actually need which, in principle, is not a good security practice.

Standard Roles - When to use them: In addition to these early Oracle version standard roles, Oracle also includes many other standard roles which are created when a database instance is created. These standard roles are designed to be used to help in database administration and Oracle encourages their use.

An example of these useful predefined standard roles includes roles such as AQ_ADMINISTRATOR_ROLE. This role grants privileges to administer Advanced Queuing and it includes ENQUEUE ANY QUEUE, DEQUEUE ANY QUEUE, and MANAGE ANY QUEUE, SELECT privileges on Advanced Queuing tables and EXECUTE privileges on Advanced Queuing packages.

Various Oracle products install additional predefined roles and DBAs are encouraged to use these standard roles by Oracle.

3.4.2 Planning and Designing Roles: Users, Applications, Objects and Functionality: In sizable production databases the design and use of roles provides significant benefits in administering users. However, the design of roles does require an upfront investment in analysis of user groups, their database activity and therefore requires DBA time.

There are several steps in the process of role design:

- Analysis of an application and its objects: This involves assembling a matrix of application modules (such as Oracle forms or reports) with a spreadsheet and then determining the database objects used by each module, i.e. the views, tables, sequences etc. used by the software in each module of the application.

At each intersect of this matrix are defined the privileges needed to use each module (SELECT, INSERT, UPDATE and/or DELETE). This provides the basic data for the DBA to create a number of "Application Roles" with the appropriate object privileges. These application roles may be defined at a module level or may be defined for several related modules. New modules can be added and old modules removed as an application evolves over time.

- An analysis of user roles: This step allows a DBA to understand which job titles will be required to use which application modules. This gives rise to a matrix of application roles versus job titles. New job titles and application roles can be added and old entries removed over time.

- **Matching users to user roles:** The final step in the process of granting roles to physical users involves defining which physical users belong to a particular job title. This analysis gives rise to a matrix of physical users versus user roles. This becomes the working role management document for the DBA as new users arrive and old users leave.

With the above matrices a DBA can now build the appropriate application and user roles and then grant groups of privileges to individual users as in the following example steps. Note that this example only uses the invoices_issued_role:

Step 1: Create Application Roles:

    CREATE ROLE   INVOICES_ISSUED_ROLE;

Step 2: Grant privileges to Application Roles (in this example just the INVOICES_ISSUED_ROLE):

    GRANT   SELECT, INSERT, UPDATE, DELETE
    ON   INVOICE_HEADERS
    TO   INVOICES_ISSUED_ROLE;

    GRANT   SELECT, INSERT, UPDATE, DELETE
    ON   INVOICE_LINES
    TO   INVOICES_ISSUED_ROLE;

    GRANT   SELECT
    ON   INVOICE_SEQUENCE
    TO   INVOICES_ISSUED_ROLE;

    GRANT   SELECT
    ON   ORDER_HEADERS
    TO   INVOICES_ISSUED_ROLE;

    GRANT   SELECT
    ON   ORDER_LINES
    TO   INVOICES_ISSUED_ROLE;

Step 3: Create User Roles In this example we create just the ACCOUNTS_CLERK_ROLE:

    CREATE ROLE   ACCOUNTS_CLERK_ROLE;

Step 4: Grant Application roles (to all user roles requiring INVOICES_ISSUED_ROLE privileges)**:**

> GRANT INVOICES_ISSUED_ROLE TO
> ACCOUNTS_CLERK ROLE;
>
> GRANT INVOICES_ISSUED_ROLE TO
> ACCOUNTS_MGR_ROLE;
>
> GRANT INVOICES_ISSUED_ROLE TO
> CREDIT_CONTROL_ROLE;

Step 5: Grant user roles to physical Oracle users: Finally a DBA grants user roles to physical Oracle users:

> GRANT ACCOUNTS_CLERK ROLE to jane_scott;
>
> GRANT ACCOUNTS_CLERK ROLE to tony_blake;
>
> GRANT ACCOUNTS _MGR_ROLE to john_smith;
>
> GRANT CREDIT_CONTROL_ROLE to janice_davis;

---oOo---

4. Managing Resources with Profiles

4.1 Introduction

Excessive use of system resources such as CPU in a multi-user Oracle system by one or more users can have damaging effects on overall system performance. Clearly, it is important to the smooth running of an Oracle database that resources are allocated according to the legitimate needs of each user. One method for managing resource allocation is the use of profiles.

A profile is simply a named set of resource limits and password parameters that restrict database resources and usage for a user. A DBA can assign a single profile to each user or a single profile to many users. Assigning a profile to a user supersedes any earlier profile they are assigned. Typically, a DBA would create several profiles according to the resource needs of groups of users and assign each member of these groups the appropriate profile. Generally, in a development or small application environment resource profiles are not often used. They are of greatest use in large, high-volume, multi-user environments.

The method used to define and allocate profiles works as follows:

- Create a list of users and determine their functional role, such as Invoice Entry Clerk, Accounts Manager, etc.

- Group together functional roles of users according to the amount of resources they will need. An accounts clerk, for instance, may simply enter single invoices committing each one to the database, whereas an Accounts Manager may need to run large batch reports or auditing procedures which need large amounts of CPU, for instance, or they may need to run multiple simultaneous sessions.

- For each similar group the DBA creates a profile which sets appropriate limits for the members of that group.

- Finally the DBA allocates each user their appropriate profile.

Note: It is worth remembering that users may occasionally need more resources than their average requirement and they may inadvertently exceed their resource limits. For this reason it is wise to keep the limits quite loose. If the limits are too tight users will constantly run into resource limit errors and this will cause unnecessary support demands on the DBA group.

4.2 Creating and Altering Profiles

Profiles are created by DBA users with the CREATE PROFILE privilege. For this to be possible, note that the database initialisation parameter RESOURCE_LIMIT must be set to TRUE. Profiles can also be altered in a similar way using the ALTER PROFILE syntax.

The following is an example of the basic syntax for the CREATE PROFILE command to manage user resource limits:

```
CREATE PROFILE                  <profile_name>
LIMIT
CPU_PER_SESSION                 UNLIMITED
CPU_PER_CALL                    4000
CONNECT_TIME                    60
COMPOSITE_LIMIT                 4000000
LOGICAL_READS_PER_SESSION       DEFAULT
LOGICAL_READS_PER_CALL          1000
PRIVATE_SGA                     20K
SESSIONS_PER_USER               UNLIMITED;
```

This profile can now be allocated to a user using the CREATE USER or ALTER USER syntax described in the previous chapter.

The UNLIMITED clause indicates that there are no limits for this resource parameter. The DEFAULT clause indicates that the value in the default profile should be used. A default profile can be altered using the ALTER PROFILE syntax.

The ALTER PROFILE syntax can be used to change a profile in a similar way to change one or more resource limits:

```
ALTER PROFILE                   <profile_name>
LIMIT
CPU_PER_SESSION                 UNLIMITED
CPU_PER_CALL                    6000
CONNECT_TIME                    65
COMPOSITE_LIMIT                 5000000
LOGICAL_READS_PER_SESSION       DEFAULT
LOGICAL_READS_PER_CALL          2000
PRIVATE_SGA                     30K
SESSIONS_PER_USER               UNLIMITED;
```

4.3 Resource Limits that can be set in a Profile

The following resource limits can be defined in a profile. These should be considered when creating groups of users defined according to their functional and resource requirements:

- SESSIONS_PER_USER

This is the number of concurrent sessions to which the user is limited.

Every time a user connects to a database, a session is created. Each session uses CPU time and memory on the server hosting the Oracle database. A DBA can set a resource limit for the number of sessions a user may create. If a user exceeds this limit, then Oracle will terminate and rollback the current statement and return an error message stating that the session limit has been reached. The user is permitted to perform only a COMMIT or ROLLBACK which is applied to the previous statements already executed. If the user chooses to disconnect the current transaction is committed. Any other operations in the current session will generate an error.

- CPU_PER_SESSION

This is the CPU time limit (in hundredths of a second) for a single session.

When SQL statements and other types of calls are made to the database, a certain amount of CPU time is necessary to process the call. Average calls require a small amount of CPU time. However, a SQL statement involving a large amount of data or a runaway query can potentially use a large amount of CPU time, reducing CPU time available for other processing.

To prevent such uncontrolled use of CPU time, a DBA can set limits on the CPU time for each call and the total amount of CPU time used for Oracle Database calls during a session.

- CPU_PER_CALL

This is the CPU time limit for a call (a parse, execute, or fetch), in hundredths of a second.

- CONNECT_TIME

This is the limit on the amount of the total elapsed time for a session which can be defined, and it is expressed in minutes. If the duration of a session exceeds this elapsed time limit, then the current transaction is rolled back, the session is dropped, and the resources of the session are returned to the system.

- IDLE_TIME

This is the limit on the continuous inactive time during a session which can be defined, and it is expressed in elapsed minutes. If the time between calls in a session reaches this idle time limit, then the current transaction is rolled back, the session is terminated, and the resources of the session are returned to the system. The next call from the user receives an error that indicates that the user is no longer connected to the database instance. Long-running queries and other operations are not subject to this idle time limit.

- LOGICAL_READS_PER_SESSION

Input and output (I/O) is one of the most resource "expensive" operations in a database system. SQL statements can be very I/O-intensive and can monopolize memory and disk use. This causes other database operations to compete for the same resources and reduces overall system performance. In order to prevent a single source of excessive I/O, a user's profile can limit the logical data block reads for each call (see LOGICAL_READS_PER_CALL) and for each session. Logical data block reads include data block reads from both memory and disk. The limits are set in terms of the number of block reads performed by a call or during a session.

- LOGICAL_READS_PER_CALL

As for LOGICAL_READS_PER_SESSION, the profile can limit the permitted number of data blocks read for a call to process a SQL statement (during a parse, execute, or fetch).

- PRIVATE_SGA

A profile can limit the amount of private System Global Area (SGA) space (used for private SQL areas) for a session. This limit is only relevant in Oracle systems that use the shared server configuration. In other cases private SQL areas are located in the Program Global Area (PGA). The private space for a session in the SGA includes private SQL and PL/SQL areas, but not shared SQL and PL/SQL areas.

The private SGA limit is set as a number of bytes of memory in the SGA of an instance. The characters K or M are used to specify kilobytes or megabytes.

- COMPOSITE_LIMIT

This profile resource limit specifies the total resource cost for a session, expressed in service units. Oracle calculates the total service units as a weighted sum of CPU_PER_SESSION, CONNECT_TIME, LOGICAL_READS_PER_SESSION, and PRIVATE_SGA.

4.3.1 Establishing Appropriate Limits for Resources: Setting resource limits too tightly will cause excessive user errors even when users are carrying out legitimate tasks. Setting limits too loosely creates the risk that system resources are wasted and system performance is degraded by careless or malicious users. Therefore it is important to set realistic limits to resources usage. Establishing realistic limits for particular groups of users can be a challenge for the average DBA, but there are ways of establishing reasonable values.

Before setting the resource limits and creating profiles, the DBA should conduct some monitoring of resource usage for each resource limit being planned. Gathering historical information of resource usage over a long period can provide invaluable insight into resource demand for each user and group. There are various means of gathering these data and several tools exist to assist in this. For example, the DBA can use the AUDIT SESSION clause to gather information about the limits CONNECT_TIME, LOGICAL_READS_PER_SESSION of users. The DBA can also gather statistics for other resource limits using the "Monitor" feature of Oracle Enterprise Manager, specifically the Statistics monitor. The data collected for real user resource demands can then be applied (normally with an extra margin of error) to define resource profiles for each resource limit parameter.

---o0o---

5. Managing Passwords with Profiles

Profiles can also be used to define how a user's password is set and define various parameters concerning the validity and lifespan of a password. A DBA should develop a consistent policy for passwords which is in line with the organisational security standards. Overtly complex password rules will cause inconvenience and annoyance to users but lack of sophistication in rules for passwords risks the user's and the system's security. A balance between password usability and complexity is required.

5.1 Creating and Altering Password Profiles

A profile with password parameters is created or altered using the CREATE PROFILE or ALTER PROFILE syntax. Here are examples of the syntax:

```
CREATE PROFILE   new_profile
LIMIT            PASSWORD_REUSE_MAX   3
                 PASSWORD_REUSE_TIME  10;
ALTER PROFILE    old_profile
LIMIT            PASSWORD_REUSE_MAX   8
                 PASSWORD_REUSE_TIME  40;
```

5.2 Password Parameters in Profiles

The following are password parameters that may be used in a profile:

- FAILED_LOGIN_ATTEMPTS

This parameter specifies a limit for the number of failed attempts to log in to the user account before the account is locked. The default in Oracle 11g is 10 failed attempts.

- PASSWORD_LIFE_TIME

This parameter specifies the number of days that the same password can be used to login to Oracle. If this parameter is set and the DBA also sets a value for the parameter PASSWORD_GRACE_TIME, then the password will expire if it is not altered within this grace period, and all connection attempts will fail. If the DBA does not set a value for PASSWORD_GRACE_TIME, then its default is UNLIMITED. This causes Oracle to issue a warning to the user but allows the user to continue to connect indefinitely. These parameters are expressed in days but can also be specified in minutes (n/1440) or even seconds (n/86400).

- -PASSWORD_GRACE_TIME

This parameter specifies the number of days after the grace period begins during which a warning is issued and login is allowed. If the password is not changed during the grace period, the password expires. See PASSWORD_LIFE_TIME.

- PASSWORD_REUSE_TIME and PASSWORD_REUSE_MAX

These two parameters are set in conjunction with each other. The parameter PASSWORD_REUSE_TIME sets the number of days before which a password cannot be reused. PASSWORD_REUSE_MAX specifies the number of password changes required before the current password can be reused. Both parameters are specified using an integer value. If specified in a profile, then the user cannot reuse a password until the password has been changed the number of times specified for PASSWORD_REUSE_MAX during the number of days specified for PASSWORD_REUSE_TIME.

For instance, if the DBA defines PASSWORD_REUSE_TIME to 20 and PASSWORD_REUSE_MAX to 5, then the user can reuse the password after 20 days if the password has already been changed 5 times.

If a value is defined for either of these parameters and the value UNLIMITED is used for the other parameter, then the user can never reuse a password. If the value of DEFAULT is used for either parameter, then Oracle uses the value defined in the DEFAULT profile (by default, all parameters are set to UNLIMITED in the DEFAULT profile). If both parameters are set to UNLIMITED, then Oracle ignores both parameters.

- PASSWORD_LOCK_TIME

This parameter defines the number of days that an account is locked after the specified number of consecutive failed login attempts.

- PASSWORD_VERIFY_FUNCTION

The PASSWORD_VERIFY_FUNCTION parameter allows a PL/SQL password complexity verification script to be passed as an argument to the CREATE PROFILE statement. Oracle provides a default script, but a DBA can also create a tailored PL/SQL routine using the CREATE FUNCTION syntax. For the function's value, the DBA uses the name of the password complexity verification function that he creates. NULL indicates that no password verification is performed. The following example shows a typical password verification function and profile where several parameters are set and the function called:

```
CREATE OR REPLACE FUNCTION pw_check

(inc_username IN VARCHAR2,

new_password IN VARCHAR2,

old_password IN VARCHAR2)

RETURN BOOLEAN

AS

password_is_good BOOLEAN;

BEGIN

--
**************************************************

-- write your own password validation code here

--
**************************************************

IF new_password = inc_username THEN

RAISE_APPLICATION_ERROR(-20001, 'Password cannot be the user name.');

END IF;

RETURN TRUE;

END password_check_function;

CREATE    PROFILE new_profile
LIMIT     FAILED_LOGIN_ATTEMPTS        3
          PASSWORD_LOCK_TIME           1
          PASSWORD_LIFE_TIME           120
          PASSWORD_GRACE_TIME          10
          PASSWORD_VERIFY_FUNCTION;    pw_check;
```

---o0o---

6. Special Users and their Privileges - SYS, SYSTEM, SYSDBA and SYSOPER

6.1 The SYS and SYSTEM Schemas

These are real schemas (users) created when the database is created. Both users are highly privileged and, generally speaking, should not be used to routinely connect to an Oracle instance even by a DBA.

- **SYS:** All base tables and views for the database data dictionary are stored in the SYS schema. These base tables and views are critical for the operations of the Oracle database. Tables in the SYS schema are manipulated automatically only by the database in order to guarantee the integrity of the database. Objects in the SYS schema must never be modified by any user or DBA. Also tables should never be created in the SYS schema. This account can perform all administrative functions of an Oracle database.

- **SYSTEM:** This account can perform all administrative functions except backup and recovery and database upgrade.

    It is possible to use this account to perform routine administrative tasks but Oracle strongly recommends creating named user accounts for administering the database or to enable monitoring of database activity rather than using the SYSTEM user.

6.2 SYSDBA and SYSOPER

These are very special and powerful system privileges used to perform high-level database administrative operations such as creating, starting up, shutting down, backing up, or recovering the database (see list in Appendix 2).

The SYSDBA system privilege is normally only granted to database administrators who have the highest level of database privilege, whereas the SYSOPER system privilege allows a database administrative user to perform basic operational tasks, but not to look at user data.

Both the SYSDBA and SYSOPER privileges allow access to a database instance, even when the database is not open because control of these privileges is completely outside the database itself. This enables an administrator who is granted one of these privileges to connect to the database instance to start up the database.

The SYS user is automatically granted the SYSDBA privilege upon installation. If a DBA connects to a database as user SYS, then they must connect to the database as either SYSDBA or SYSOPER. Connecting as SYSDBA user invokes the SYSDBA privilege; connecting as SYSOPER invokes the SYSOPER privilege, as follows:

SQL> connect SYS/<password> as SYSDBA

6.2.1 Granting SYSDBA or SYSOPER to a User: Obviously only a highly privileged senior DBA should ever be granted SYSDBA because it basically gives them access to the SYS schema which holds the Oracle data dictionary. The SYSDBA privilege can only be granted when connected as SYS or SYSTEM as in the following example:

- Connect to the database as user SYS:

　　　SQL> connect SYS/<password> as SYSDBA

- Grant the SYSDBA or SYSOPER system privilege to the user:

　　　SQL>GRANT SYSDBA to <username>;

6.2.2 Connecting as SYSDBA or SYSOPER: A user that has been granted SYSDBA or SYSOPER connects to the database in the normal way but can specify which privilege to connect with:

　　　SQL>connect <username>/<password> as SYSDBA;

When connected in this way with the SYSDBA or SYSOPER privilege, the user is connected with a default schema, not with their own schema associated with their user name. For SYSDBA this default schema is SYS; for SYSOPER the default schema is PUBLIC. Therefore a user connected as SYSDBA sees objects in the SYS schema and not their own schema.

Note: Oracle Enterprise Manager Database Control does not permit a user to log in as user SYS without connecting as either SYSDBA or SYSOPER.

---o0o---

7. Managing Developer Security

The management of security in a software development environment is somewhat different to that of a stable production database. Development users have special needs which do not apply to users of a finished production application. For instance, development users such as designers may need to create and alter tables and other database objects in order to design, build and test new software modules. Therefore they may require extensive system privileges such as ALTER TABLE which a normal production user would absolutely not require or be granted. In general, ordinary application users are only ever granted object privileges whereas developers are typically granted both object privileges and some system privileges.

7.1 Working on a Single Schema Version

One major consideration in a software development environment is that all developers are working on the latest version of the schema for the application being developed. Ideally, a development database schema should be stable before software development begins but in reality changes to database object designs are often required after software development has begun.

Ad-hoc alterations to a schema may well cause software to fail and uncontrolled schema changes can damage an application's functionality, cause a loss of effort and induce a very chaotic development environment where developers are unsure of whether they have produced software against a valid schema.

For this reason, care must be taken to ensure that schema change control is very carefully managed. This means that a separate group within the development team should be responsible for maintaining the schema in a considered way with a clear methodology for managing change. These custodians of the application schema(s) are therefore the only development users that are usually granted any system privileges to create or alter database objects. Ideally, schema design should be centrally managed using a tool such as Oracle Designer, SQL Developer Data Modeller or one of the many third-party design tools available.

Thus, when schema changes are proposed, these changes need to be evaluated for their impact on an application being developed. There are many tools available to carry out such an impact analysis. In general, when a schema change is made, it is imperative to implement the change in a copy of the working schema and carefully test its effects before rolling out the changes into the live development schema. For this reason the development schema "custodians" (often referred to as "development DBAs") need various system privileges on one or more copy test schemas. When the schema changes are tested and approved in the copy schema they can then be rolled out into the main development schema and republished to the development team.

7.2 Software Developer Security

Generally speaking, software developers should not have any system privileges to alter or create objects in the main development schema. However, they will need enough privilege to create procedures, functions, packages, etc. in order to design and build their application software. This is usually managed by allowing developers to create procedures, functions, packages, etc. within their own schema and execute them against the main schema or a test schema which is frequently refreshed with test data and any schema changes which are implemented centrally by development DBAs.

In some cases it is also necessary to allow developers to create copies of the latest development schema in their own schema. Clearly, developers require extensive object privileges to test their software against the latest development schema. This, however, raises an issue when a group of developers are simultaneously designing, building and testing software against a single schema because of the risk of multiple developers carrying out DML operations against the same tables, which could easily give rise to confusing results as data are simultaneously modified by multiple developers.

In general, this problem is managed by permitting developers to create local copies of an application schema (or part of it) under their own schema. This may well involve importing a data populated schema or part of a schema to a developers schema. In large development environments this involves creating daily or weekly data-populated exports of a clean, up-to-date development schema. In such environments a local "development DBA" would be responsible for creating these exports and making them available along with the necessary scripts to allow developers to "refresh" their local copies at will.

Another issue is that very often a local copy of a schema being used by a developer becomes corrupted by intensive testing and needs to be refreshed. Therefore the process of dropping a schema copy and importing a clean copy needs to be streamlined and flexible.

Developers also therefore need the necessary privileges to DROP objects and to IMPORT and CREATE the fresh schema objects from the central development schema. Developers (in general) do not need any privileges to ALTER objects and they should not be granted any privilege with ADMIN or GRANT option and they should not be given system privileges with the ANY option.

7.3 RAD Development Environment

Some exceptions to the restrictions for developer security mentioned above may be made in a RAD (Rapid Application Development) environment. A RAD methodology does not follow the traditional, long-cycle, so-called "waterfall" or "cascade" path of analysis-design-build. On the contrary, it relies on very short-cycle prototyping of database and software.

In a Rapid Application Development environment, the designer is often also the developer. The use of short-cycle prototyping means that the designer-developer needs a lot of object and system privileges to create and alter database objects as well as writing application code, more or less at will. Depending on the size of the development, the size of the development team and the frequency of prototype releases, a developer may have almost limitless object and system privilege within a very controlled environment.

---o0o---

8. Virtual Private Databases (VPD)

A virtual private database (VPD) provides a means by which access to data may be controlled at a row and column level. This is done by means of a so-called VPD "policy" associated with a table (or view or synonym) and these policies provide a very useful means of allowing strong, "fine-grained" data security within one or more tables.

A policy defines how data can be accessed from within a particular object (such as a table or view) and, most importantly, a policy is defined WITHIN the schema rather than externally, such as similar row-level security techniques defined within external application software, for instance. A policy is therefore a very secure, object-level method of securing data.

For instance, a database which stores data belonging to and accessed by many separate private client users could employ the same database and a single schema but may be divided into many "virtual private databases" using this technology to securely separate data from many clients. The benefits of this approach are obvious:

- Security can be defined at an object level rather than within an application (an application may NOT be a user's only access method to a schema and therefore security cannot be guaranteed). This means that however a user accesses a table a VPD policy absolutely guarantees the limits of their access to data.

- VPD Policies are very flexible and can be defined at a DML level, with different policies for SELECT, INSERT, UPDATE and DELETE.

- A VPD policy is defined for a table (or view or synonym) once only and no application changes are necessary. The same application software may be used by all users using the same tables and access is seamlessly controlled by the VPD policies defined on these underlying tables.

8.1 How do VPD Policies work?

A VPD policy dynamically and transparently modifies the underlying SQL statement issued by a user by adding a predicate (WHERE clause) built into the policy. This predicate appending the SQL is based on a function implementing the policy. Any condition that can be expressed in or returned by a function may be used. This provides a powerful and secure method of dynamically and safely limiting access to data based

50

on the user or other context information for example, using the SYS_CONTEXT function.

The SYS_CONTEXT function can be used to return a wealth of information about the current Oracle session, including the current user id, and this can be leveraged to provide a layer of very granular data security at a user or higher level.

For instance, in a case where several users use the same schema to store their orders, we might want to restrict the access of a particular user so that they can view and maintain just the orders that they created. But our order entry application executes the following SQL:

```
SELECT   *
FROM     ORDER_HEADERS;
```

This would return all ORDER_HEADERS rows for all users. In this example, what we really want to do is to have SQL return just the current user's ORDER_HEADERS as follows (user is '12345'):

```
SELECT   *
FROM     ORDER_HEADERS
WHERE    CUSTOMER= '12345';
```

Using a policy we can implement this using the application context of

```
SELECT   *
FROM     ORDER_HEADERS
WHERE    CUSTOMER=
         SYS_CONTEXT('USERENV','SESSION_USER');
```

With such a VPD policy, regardless of who attempts to access the ORDER_HEADERS table they will only be able to see the ORDER records that belong to them and no other records.

8.1.1 Advantages of Virtual Private Databases (VPD): Virtual private databases provide a very strong method of guaranteeing data security based on a wide, flexible range of parameters.

Most importantly, VPD is implemented at the database level and not at the application level. This provides an easy to maintain but very reliable form of data security because regardless of how the data is accessed the rules embedded in the VPD policy are always enforced. Here are some more advantages:

- Multiple security policies - Using VPD, a developer can place more than one security policy on each object (table, view or synonym), as well as adding highly-specific policies alongside more basic policies such as the user access control in the above example.

- Good for Web applications - Many web applications use a single Oracle user to connect to the database and this can make user-driven data filtering a challenge. However, row-level security with VPD can easily differentiate between users using various values about their real (non-Oracle) user's id.

- No back-doors with VPD - In the past, security mechanisms were often embedded in application software because these applications frequently used a single Oracle user to address the database. However, when using VPD, the control of data access is brought back to the database end of the application and is not embedded within the application software. This means that users can no longer bypass security mechanisms embedded in an application, because the security is attached directly to the database by means of a VPD policy.

8.2 Creating a Policy

Once you have made the decision to use VPD technology, then policies are designed and created as part of the design of the database. Clearly, in the example above, the ORDER_HEADERS table needs a column which contains the user id. Therefore these considerations obviously affect the database design.

However, once these design issues have been implemented, the creation of table policies are a "one-off" DDL process which is normally built into a script and runs once after all schema objects are created. No further application changes or DDL are required. The policy effectively becomes part of the table definition.

There are many ways of implementing policies depending on the application requirements. For instance, data may be flagged by the user id of the creator, or it may be flagged with a company or client id, the id of a sales representative or employee, whatever is required to filter data. Depending on the functional requirements, policies can be used in conjunction with other tables and application contexts to provide a seamless layer of data security.

Policies are created using the PL/SQL package called DBMS_RLS. The most important procedures within this package are as follows:

- DBMS_RLS.ADD_POLICY - This is used to create a new policy

- DBMS_RLS.DROP_POLICY - This is used to drop an existing policy

8.2.1 The Basic Syntax to Add a Policy is as follows:

```
DBMS_RLS.ADD_POLICY (
OBJECT_SCHEMA              IN VARCHAR2 NULL
OBJECT_NAME               IN VARCHAR2
POLICY_NAME               IN VARCHAR2
FUNCTION_SCHEMA           IN VARCHAR2 NULL
POLICY_FUNCTION           IN VARCHAR2
STATEMENT_TYPES           IN VARCHAR2 NULL          .
UPDATE_CHECK              IN BOOLEAN  FALSE
ENABLE                    IN BOOLEAN  TRUE
STATIC_POLICY             IN BOOLEAN  FALSE
POLICY_TYPE               IN BINARY_INTEGER NULL
LONG_PREDICATE            IN BOOLEAN  FALSE
SEC_RELEVANT_COLS         IN VARCHAR2 NULL
SEC_RELEVANT_COLS_OPT     IN BINARY_INTEGER NULL);
```

Most of this syntax is unused in many databases and we will confine ourselves to examples employing the most useful clauses. But for completeness, here are the explanations for each of these parameters:

- OBJECT_SCHEMA: The schema containing the table, view, or synonym. If no object_schema is specified, the current user's schema is assumed.

- OBJECT_NAME: The name of table, view, or synonym to which the policy is added.

- POLICY_NAME: The name of policy to be added. This must be unique for the same table or view.

- FUNCTION_SCHEMA: The schema of the policy function. If no function_schema is specified, the current user's schema is assumed.

- POLICY_FUNCTION: The name of a function which generates a predicate for the policy. If the function is defined within a package, then the name of the package must also be specified.

- STATEMENT_TYPES: The statement types to which the policy applies. It can be any combination of INDEX, SELECT, INSERT, UPDATE, or DELETE. The default is to apply the policy to all statement types except INDEX.

- UPDATE_CHECK: This is an optional argument for INSERT or UPDATE statement types. The default is FALSE. Setting update_check to TRUE causes the server to also check the policy against the value after INSERT or UPDATE. The purpose of this argument is to restrict updates (or inserts) that would lead to updated or inserted rows to fall out of the allowed visibility for a particular user, for example by attempting to update the user_id of a record when a policy function uses this column (user_id) as a means of generating a predicate.

- ENABLE: This indicates if the policy is enabled when it is added. The default is TRUE.

- STATIC_POLICY: The default for this value is FALSE. If it is set to TRUE, the server assumes that the policy function for the policy produces the same predicate string for anyone accessing the object, except for SYS or the privileged user who has the EXEMPT ACCESS POLICY privilege.

- POLICY_TYPE: The default is NULL. This means policy_type is decided by the value of static_policy. The available policy types are listed below in the section on "performance considerations when using a VPD". Specifying any of these policy types overrides the value of static_policy.

- LONG_PREDICATE: The default is FALSE, which means the policy function can return a predicate with a length of up to 4000 bytes. TRUE means the predicate text string length can be up to 32K bytes. The policies which existed before the availability of this parameter have a 32K limit.

- SEC_RELEVANT_COLS: This enables column-level VPD, which enforces security policies when a column containing sensitive information is referenced in a query. This applies to tables and views, but not to synonyms. To use this, it is necessary to specify a list of comma or space separated column names from the policy-protected object (table or view). The policy is enforced only if one of the specified columns is referenced in a SQL statement or its underlying view definition. The default is that ALL the user-defined columns for the object are relevant.

- SEC_RELEVANT_COLS_OPT: This argument is used with the sec_relevant_cols parameter to display all rows for column-level VPD filtered queries (SELECT only), but where sensitive columns appear as NULL. The default is set to NULL, which allows the filtering defined with sec_relevant_cols to take effect. Set to dbms_rls.ALL_ROWS to display all rows, but with sensitive column values, which are filtered by sec_relevant_cols, displayed as NULL.

Here is an example ADD_POLICY statement:

```
EXECUTE    DBMS_RLS.ADD_POLICY
              ('USER_1',
              'PURCHASE_ORDERS',
              'PURCHASE_ORDERS_SEC_1');
              'USER_1',
              'FUNCTION1'
              'INSERT,UPDATE,
              DELETE,SELECT');
```

In this example, the policy is called 'PURCHASE_ORDERS_SEC_1'. It is created in the schema USER_1 on the table (or view or synonym) called PURCHASE_ORDERS and it adds the predicate returned by FUNCTION1 (also in the schema USER_1). This predicate is used in all INSERT, UPDATE, DELETE, and SELECT statements on this table.

8.2.2 The Basic Syntax to Drop a Policy is as follows:

```
DBMS_RLS.DROP_POLICY(
OBJECT_SCHEMA            IN VARCHAR2 NULL
OBJECT_NAME             IN VARCHAR2
POLICY_NAME             IN VARCHAR2);
```

OBJECT_NAME is the table, view or synonym and POLICY_NAME is the name of the existing policy on that object.

For instance, the following statement will drop the policy called 'PURCHASE_ORDERS_SEC_1' on the table 'PURCHASE_ORDERS' which is owned by user 'USER_1':

```
EXECUTE
DBMS_RLS.DROP_POLICY    ('USER_1',
                         'PURCHASE_ORDERS',
                         'PURCHASE_ORDERS_SEC_1');
```

8.3 Creating a Function to Generate the Dynamic WHERE clause used in a VPD policy.

To generate the dynamic WHERE clause in a VPD policy, it is necessary to create a function that defines the restrictions that you want to enforce in a predicate. Usually, a DBA will create this function in the application schema (as owner) but it can also be created in another schema. Of course, there can also be several functions used by different policies in any combination.

The purpose of the function is to generate the predicate to be used by the VPD policy. For instance, the function may return a string such as 'USER_ID = <current_user>'. It isn't necessary to generate the 'where' part of the conditional clause in the function, simply the condition itself. Obviously, there are many possible predicate clauses that a function can be made to generate depending on the application.

Here is a simple typical function which creates a predicate based on the current session user:

```
CREATE OR REPLACE FUNCTION MY_ORDERS
(SCHEMA IN VARCHAR2,
TAB IN VARCHAR2)
RETURN VARCHAR2
IS
V_USER VARCHAR2(100);
OUT_STRING VARCHAR2(400);
BEGIN
V_USER :=
LOWER(SYS_CONTEXT('USERENV','SESSION_USER'));
OUT_STRING:= OUT_STRING||' USER_ID ='||V_USER;
RETURN OUT_STRING;
END;
```

In this example, when this function is implemented into a VPD policy against the ORDER_HEADERS table, a session user 'jsmith' would only be able to see records where the table column USER_ID is equal to 'jsmith'.

8.3.1 Rules for Constructing VPD functions: In all cases, the function created must conform to the following rules:

1. A function must accept as input arguments i/ a schema name and ii/ an object (usually a table but this can also be a view, or synonym). In the example above these are the input parameters:

- SCHEMA IN

- TAB IN

The schema and object name should not be explicitly defined within the function because when the policy itself is created, the DBMS_RLS package passes the names of the schema and object to which the policy will apply to the associated function.

2. The function must define the input parameter for the schema first, followed by the parameter for the object because this is the order in which the DBMS_RLS package passes these parameters.

3 The function must provide a return value for the WHERE clause predicate as a VARCHAR2 data type and without the 'WHERE'. In the example function above, the generated predicate looks like this:

' USER_ID ='|V_USER

Where V_USER becomes equal to the Oracle current session user such as 'jsmith'.

Obviously, the generated predicate must be valid SQL for a WHERE clause. The full SQL syntax is available to construct a WHERE clause predicate in the function as would be done in normal SQL.

8.3.2 Using a VPD Function to create Dynamic Predicates: In the example above we used session information about the current user to dynamically alter the construction of the predicates used by the VPD policy. Thus if jsmith is connected the predicate becomes:

USER_ID ='jmsith'

If pscott is connected the predicate becomes:

USER_ID ='pscott'

This dynamic predicate is accomplished by using a so-called application context within the function. In the example above the function sets the variable v_user to be equal to the current SESSION_USER using the following syntax:

V_USER :=   LOWER(SYS_CONTEXT
('USERENV','SESSION_USER'));

There are many application context values which Oracle stores in memory and which can be retrieved and used in a VPD function.

The employment of such application context values is extremely useful because it means that functions return context sensitive predicates to the VPD. In this way the VPD can be designed to restrict access to data owned by or created by a specific user or, with a little extra code, the current user data can be used to restrict access to sets of data of a particular department or client associated with a user. The possibilities of using application contexts in a VPD are limitless.

Of course, a function used by a VPD doesn't have to use application context values to generate the predicate. Literal values can be used but the use of application context values provides a totally secure way of limiting data access.

In addition to using application context values in a function to generate the predicate clause, a developer can also embed C or Java calls to access operating system information or to return WHERE clauses from an operating system file or other source.

One important (and obvious) restriction is that a function cannot select from a table within the associated policy function. Although we can define a policy against a table, we cannot select from that table from within the policy that was defined against the table.

8.4 Performance Considerations when using a VPD

Using VPD can affect performance if the associated functions are run many times. If functions perform SQL queries and the functions need to be constantly run then obviously there are cases when unnecessary calls are being made to the database.

Oracle solves this problem by allowing the predicates generated by the VPD to be cached. Thus, a developer can optimize performance each time a policy runs by specifying a policy type for their policies.

Policy types control how the Oracle Database caches Oracle Virtual Private Database policy predicates. Therefore one should consider setting a policy type for the defined policies, because the execution of policy functions can use a significant amount of system resources. Minimizing the number of times that a policy function runs optimizes database performance. These types enable the developer to precisely specify how often a policy predicate should change. To specify the policy type the developer set the policy_type parameter of the DBMS_RLS.ADD POLICY procedure.

There are five policy types:

- DYNAMIC - The DYNAMIC policy type runs the policy function each time a user accesses the Virtual Private Database-protected database objects. This policy type does not optimize database performance.

- STATIC - The static policy type enforces the same predicate for all users in the instance. Oracle Database stores static policy predicates in SGA (memory), so policy functions do not rerun for each query. This means that no matter which user accesses the objects, everyone gets the same predicate. Static policy functions are executed once and then cached in SGA memory. This results in better performance. Static policies are ideal for environments where every query requires the same predicate and high performance is essential. If you set the policy_type parameter in the dbms_rls.add_policy procedure to static, the policy is applied to a single object.

- SHARED_STATIC - As for STATIC, but if you set the policy_type parameter to shared_static, the policy is applied to multiple objects.

- CONTEXT_SENSITIVE and SHARED_CONTEXT_SENSITIVE - Context-sensitive policies do not always cache the predicate. With context-sensitive policies, the database assumes that the predicate may change after statement parse time. But if there is no change in the application context, Oracle Database does not rerun the policy function within the user session. If there was a change in context, then the database does rerun the policy function to ensure that it embodies any changes to the predicate since the last parsing. Context-sensitive policies are useful when a predicate does not need to change for a user session, but the policy must enforce two or more different predicates for different users or groups.

---o0o---

9. Procedure Execution Security

One limitation of traditional role-based security is that end-users can bypass their application screens and access their granted Oracle database objects using other tools such as SQL*Plus or other third party products. The object and data privileges they have are available to them regardless of the tool or access method and this uncontrolled access may be undesirable.

However, Oracle provides another method of enforcing object and data security without using the conventional role-based techniques for managing object privileges and this is referred to as the GRANT EXECUTE model. It is an entirely different approach to the use of database object privileges.

In this GRANT EXECUTE scenario users have very limited privileges which basically allow them to execute certain database procedures (PL/SQL or Java). They don't need or receive DML privileges on any database tables or views because all the privileges they need are encapsulated in the database privileges to which the users are granted the EXECUTE privilege. In many cases, the "grant execute" security method provides tighter control of access security because it controls not only those database entities that a person is able to see, but what they're able to do with those entities.

Using the "grant execute" method, the individual user needs nothing more than CONNECT privileges to attach to the Oracle database. Once attached, execution privileges on any given stored procedure, package, or function are directly granted to each user. At runtime, the user is able to execute one or more procedures, and gains the privileges of the owner of that procedure.

9.1 Advantages of the GRANT EXECUTE Method

There are several benefits in putting SQL inside stored procedures and these include:

- **Improved security:** In this scenario, users are not granted any explicit privileges against the database. The DBA only grants the necessary object privileges to the application owner but NOT the users. The users are then granted EXECUTE privilege on the procedures owned by the application owner and the only way that users can access the data is by using the granted procedures. This gives the DBA and system owners complete access control of which data the user can see and how they can manipulate these data. This provides a much stronger level of data security than data specific security granted to each user. In this scenario there is no possibility of end-users accessing tables from other packages or using other tools or applications.

The "grant execute" method has its greatest benefit in the coupling of data access security and procedural security. When an individual end user is granted execute privileges against a stored procedure or package, the end-user may use those packages only within the context of the application itself. This has the additional benefit of enforcing table-level security, but also column-level security. Inside the PL/SQL package, the application owner can specify individual WHERE predicates based on the user id and very tightly control their access to virtually any distinct data item within the database.

- **Isolation of code:** In this model all SQL is moved out of the external application software and placed in stored procedures. In this way the application software becomes no more than a means of calling the stored procedures and in this way the database becomes independent of the application.

- **Better performance:** Stored procedures load just once into the shared pool of the database and remain there until they become paged out because of non-use. This improves performance by reducing the need for continuous parsing of SQL. The stored procedures can also be aggregated into packages, which can then be pinned inside the Oracle SGA which greatly improves performance.

- **Ease of administration:** In this case, the owner of the procedures controls all the access rights to the database. Therefore there is no necessity to create and maintain large user and role GRANT scripts for each any every end-user. This greatly reduces database and user administration.

- **Modularisation and Object Orientation:** By coupling data with behaviour in database procedures, the developers can modularise their design to associate tables with the behaviours directly associated with that table. This is in line with the design concept of producing object-oriented code. The "grant execute" security model fits in very well with the objective of producing modular object-oriented software by moving all business logic into the database where it can be closely associated with that particular database and simultaneously provide additional security. In this way, the database becomes the repository not only for the data itself, but for all of the SQL, stored procedures and functions that are used to transform the data.

9.2 Disadvantages of the GRANT EXECUTE Method

One minor problem in using the grant execute method is that the end-user's access to database objects is controlled by the database procedures and it is therefore not possible to easily see which users have what accesses based on the usual data dictionary tables that store access rights. Therefore a DBA and system owner will have to initially explicitly document the database object privileges given by a particular package and then record which users have access to which packages. However, this is a relatively easy exercise to carry out after an application is developed and shouldn't be seen as an obstacle to using this methodology.

---o0o---

10. Data Security using Views

When we use complete row-level security measures such as VPD, we are actually creating an environment where Oracle builds transient views of our data based on static or dynamic predicates generated by one or more functions associated with security policies on one or more tables. These "transient" views act to filter data based on some context value such as the current logged-in user. VPD provides a very safe and flexible way to provide dynamic or static data filtering security.

However, before the advent of VPD a similar (though less flexible and dynamic) method of filtering data could be achieved using ordinary Oracle views. This simple method of filtering data is still available to the Oracle developer and may be quite appropriate in the design of certain types of application. In this methodology it is possible to build up a range of static views of any number of tables based on some specific column value (which is within a fixed range of known values) and safely grant access to these views to specific users or roles.

For many purposes, the use of views to manage some aspects of data security is quite adequate, very secure and somewhat simpler than using a VPD. However it is also more limited.

10.1 Filtering Row-level Data based on a Column value using a Ciew

A simple example shows how personnel data can be row and column filtered by creating a series of static views which can then be granted to specific interested parties:

```
CREATE VIEW    FINANCE_EMPS_1
AS
SELECT         *
FROM           EMPS
WHERE          DEPT = 'FINANCE';
GRANT          SELECT
ON             FINANCE_EMPS_1
TO             FINANCE_ROLE_1;
```

Here we first create a view of all employee columns called FINANCE_EMPS_1 where employees work for the FINANCE department. We then grant SELECT privilege to a role used for certain FINANCE users called FINANCE_ROLE_1. In this way, users who belong to the FINANCE_ROLE_1 role will see all EMP data but only the employees from the department FINANCE.

10.2 Filtering Row and Column-level data based on a Column value using a View

We can further filter column and row data in another view:

```
CREATE VIEW   FINANCE_EMPS_2
AS
SELECT        EMP_ID,
              NAME,
              POSITION
FROM          EMPS
WHERE         DEPT = 'FINANCE';
GRANT         SELECT
ON            FINANCE_EMPS_2
TO            FINANCE_ROLE_2;
```

Here we have filtered out all but FINANCE department employees and the view FINANCE_EMPS_2 only includes the columns EMP_ID, NAME and POSITION. We can then grant SELECT access to the role FINANCE_ROLE_2. In this way, users who belong to the FINANCE_ROLE_2 role will see only selected columns from the EMP table (EMP_ID, NAME, POSITION) and only see rows of data for employees from the department FINANCE.

10.3 Context-sensitive Filtering using Static Views

Using static views to filter rows and columns can be made quite sophisticated. For instance, date ranges can be included in a view. More interestingly pseudo columns such as SYSDATE and USER can also be incorporated into the view construction, thus giving some measure of dynamic control over the data returned by the view:

For example, we can create a view which uses the USER pseudo column to filter rows based on the user which SELECTs from the view. For instance, we could first create the view of the EMP table:

```
CREATE VIEW   USER_EMP
AS
SELECT        *
FROM          EMP
WHERE         ENAME=USER;
```

This creates a view where the rows returned match only where ENAME equals the currently logged in USER (the pseudo column USER always returns the current user). The user SCOTT then connects and executes a query as follows:

```
SELECT    *
FROM      USER_EMP;
```

In this case SCOTT will see only his own data where ENAME= 'SCOTT'.

Further refinements using pseudo columns can involve using joins and sub-queries to other tables where these pseudo columns match particular records. In this way static views can be a simple and effective way of controlling data access security.

---oOo---

11. Tool Security - PRODUCT_USER_PROFILE table

11.1 Introduction

A potential security problem exists when users have access to SQL*Plus. A user may install a client-side copy of SQL*Plus or may have been given access to SQL*Plus in order to run a fixed report. In other cases, various other products embed SQL*Plus within them and there is a potential for a user to gain direct access to tables for which they have been given privileges. This is undesirable for several reasons. Here are some examples:

- A user can build and execute a very inefficient SQL statement which may impact system performance by taking up system resources. For example, a user can easily create a script which causes a Cartesian join between two large tables and create a potentially fatal drain on server resources.

- A user may issue a range of SQL commands such as a table or row level LOCK which could LOCK rows or entire tables causing errors or even system failures for other users. Obviously, this is undesirable.

- A user may attempt to build and execute PL/SQL procedures without permission.

Clearly, there are many good reasons why a user may need to be denied access to SQL*Plus entirely or partially, where their access needs to be restricted to just some commands within the SQL syntax set.

Oracle provides a means of controlling both complete access or limiting the use of SQL*Plus and this is implemented by a DBA using the standard PRODUCT_USER_PROFILE table. This table is created during the database creation process. If it does not exist, a DBA can create it by running the script pupbld.sql in $ORACLE_HOME/sqlplus/admin directory logged in as the user SYSTEM. (Note: this script must be run as SYSTEM, not SYS.)

To disable a particular SQL or SQL*Plus command for one or more users, it is necessary to insert one or more rows into the PRODUCT_USER_PROFILE table. The table has the following structure:

PRODUCT	NOT NULL CHAR (30)
USERID	CHAR(30)
ATTRIBUTE	CHAR(240)
SCOPE	CHAR(240)
NUMERIC_VALUE	NUMBER(15,2)
CHAR_VALUE	CHAR(240)
DATE_VALUE	DATE
LONG_VALUE	LONG

However, only the following columns are used by Oracle:

- PRODUCT - This must contain the product name - in this case "SQL*Plus", specified in mixed case.

- USERID - This field must contain the username (in uppercase) of the user for whom a command is being disabled. Wildcards (%) are permitted.

- ATTRIBUTE - This field must contain the name (in uppercase) of the SQL command you wish to disable, e.g. "INSERT"

- CHAR_VALUE - This field must contain the character string "DISABLED".

11.2 Limiting Access to specific SQL*Plus Commands

In order to limit access for one or more users to specific SQL commands, the DBA inserts a row into the PRODUCT_USER_PROFILE as in the following example:

PRODUCT	USERID	ATTRIBUTE	CHAR_VALUE
SQL*Plus	SCO%	INSERT	DISABLED
SQL*Plus	USER_ID	SPOOL	DISABLED
SQL*Plus	%	UPDATE	DISABLED
SQL*Plus	%	DELETE	DISABLED

Many SQL commands can be disabled and Appendix 3 contains a complete list.

11.3 Blocking Access to SQL*Plus entirely

The PRODUCT_USER_PROFILE table provides a highly granular way of disabling specific commands for specific users. In order to disable all possible SQL commands for a specific user (or all users) it is necessary to insert multiple records into the table with each explicit command to be disabled for a user or users. This is normally accomplished with a SQL script executed by the DBA.

---o0o---

12. Obtaining Security Information from the Data Dictionary

12.1 Getting Information on User Privileges and Roles

Managing users and privileges is a vital part of the role of a DBA. It requires both an understanding of the applications using a database in which objects are accessed by each part of an application and the functional activities of each user.

To manage this task, a DBA needs easy access to the current information about all users, objects, privileges and roles. A number of Oracle data dictionary views make this relatively easy. Below we provide some example scripts to extract this information.

12.2 Data Dictionary Views That Display Information about Users and Profiles

The following data dictionary views are useful in obtaining user, privilege and role information. Generally, a DBA may maintain a set of standard scripts to extract data from these views or will use GUI tools such as Oracle Enterprise Manager or other third party tools to obtain the same data from these views. Some views are available to all users and some views are only to a DBA with appropriate privileges:

Data Dictionary Views and Description

The following data dictionary objects provide detailed information about user and object security and privileges:

- ALL_OBJECTS - Describes all objects accessible to the current user

- ALL_USERS - Lists users visible to the current user

- DBA_PROFILES - Contains all profiles and their limits

- DBA_TS_QUOTAS - Describes tablespace quotas for users

- DBA_OBJECTS - Describes all objects in the database

- DBA_SYS_PRIVS - Lists the system privileges that have been granted to a user

- DBA_USERS - Describes all users of the database

- DBA_USERS_WITH_DEFPWD - Lists all user accounts that have default passwords

- PROXY_USERS - Describes users who can assume the identity of other users

- USER_PASSWORD_LIMITS - Describes the password profile parameters that are assigned to the user

- USER_RESOURCE_LIMITS - Displays the resource limits for the current user

- USER_TS_QUOTAS - Describes tablespace quotas for users

- USER_OBJECTS - Describes all objects owned by the current user

- USER_USERS - Describes only the current user

- V$SESSION - Lists session information for each current session, includes user name

- V$SESSTAT - Lists user session statistics

- V$STATNAME - Displays decoded statistic names for the statistics shown in the V$SESSTAT view

---o0o---

13. Glossary of Terms

Database Administrator (DBA): A DBA is a special database user who has extra system privileges allowing him to manage database resources and administer other users. Various grades of DBA exist, depending on their own level of privilege. Some (junior) DBAs may be restricted to relatively routine tasks whereas other DBAs may have wide-ranging privileges which may include the right to create or drop, start and stop a database or to see and manipulate all the data in the database.

Data Dictionary: Oracle maintains a set of internal tables and views which contain a repository of the metadata which define the database. This is referred to as the "Data Dictionary". These metadata include definitions of all the database objects such as tables, users, internal processes such as locks, storage definitions, etc. The total data dictionary is generally directly accessible to query only by a DBA. However, Oracle constantly references the data dictionary when a normal end user makes a request for data. For instance, the data dictionary contains crucial security information about a user's privileges.

Database Objects (in Oracle): The phrase "database object" is used in Oracle to refer to certain data or schema objects owned by a database user. Thus a table or view is a database object, as is a database procedure, index or sequence (see Schema below).

Function (PL/SQL): A PL/SQL function is stored in the Oracle database and is similar to a procedure but always returns a value when called. Oracle provides many standard functions to carry out common tasks such as the UPPER function used in converting a string into UPPER case, but a developer can create a completely turnkey function "from scratch" to satisfy a particular application requirement.

PL/SQL: This is an acronym for "Procedural Language/Structured Query Language" which is Oracle's procedural extension for SQL. SQL is a non-procedural language and thus limited in how it can be used in application development. However, PL/SQL includes procedural language elements such as conditions and loops and it allows the declaration of constants and variables, procedures and functions, types and variables of those types, and triggers. PL/SQL is central to Oracle application development.

Package (PL/SQL): A PL/SQL package is an object which is created and stored in a database schema containing logically related PL/SQL types, items, and subprograms such as procedures. Packages provide improved modularity of software and improved execution performance.

Procedure (PL/SQL): A "PL/SQL stored procedure" is a software procedure written in PL/SQL that is stored in a database schema. A stored procedure is a named PL/SQL block which performs one or more specific tasks. This is similar to a procedure in other programming languages. A stored procedure can be executed at will by anyone granted the privilege to execute it.

Schema: A schema is a collection of logical structures of data, or schema objects. A schema is owned by a database user and has the same name as that user. Each user owns a single schema. Schema objects can be created and manipulated with SQL and include the following types of object:

- Clusters
- Constraints
- Database links
- Database triggers
- Dimensions
- External procedure libraries
- Index-organized tables
- Indexes
- Indextypes
- Java classes, Java resources, Java sources
- Materialized views
- Materialized view logs
- Object tables
- Object types
- Object views
- Operators
- Packages
- Sequences

- Stored functions, stored procedures

- Synonyms

- Tables

- Views

- System Owner

- Tablespace

SQL and SQL*Plus: SQL stands for "Structured Query Language" and is a special-purpose programming language designed for managing data held in a relational database. SQL*Plus is Oracle's own interactive and batch query tool that is installed with every Oracle Database installation. It has a command-line user interface and various Oracle and third-party GUI and web-based user interfaces.

---oOo---

Appendix 1 - Common System Privileges

The following is a list of common Oracle system privileges:

PRIVILEGE	Description
ADMIN	Enables a user to perform administrative tasks including checkpointing, backups, migration, and user creation and deletion.
ALTER ANY CACHE GROUP	Enables a user to alter any cache group in the database.
ALTER ANY INDEX	Enables a user to alter any index in the database.
ALTER ANY MATERIALIZED VIEW	Enables a user to alter any materialized view in the database.
ALTER ANY PROCEDURE	Enables a user to alter any PL/SQL procedure, function or package in the database.
ALTER ANY SEQUENCE	Enables a user to alter any sequence in the database.
ALTER ANY TABLE	Enables a user to alter any table in the database.
ALTER ANY VIEW	Enables a user to alter any view in the database.
CACHE_MANAGER	Enables a user to perform operations related to cache groups.
CREATE ANY CACHE GROUP	Enables a user to create a cache group owned by any user in the database.
CREATE ANY INDEX	Enables a user to create an index on any table or materialized view in the database.
CREATE ANY MATERIALIZED VIEW	Enables a user to create a materialized view owned by any user in the database.
CREATE ANY PROCEDURE	Enables a user to create a PL/SQL procedure, function or package owned by any user in the database.

CREATE ANY SEQUENCE	Enables a user to create a sequence owned by any user in the database.
CREATE ANY SYNONYM	Enables a user to create a private synonym owned by any user in the database.
CREATE ANY TABLE	Enables a user to create a table owned by any user in the database.
CREATE ANY VIEW	Enables a user to create a view owned by any user in the database.
CREATE CACHE GROUP	Enables a user to create a cache group owned by that user.
CREATE MATERIALIZED VIEW	Enables a user to create a materialized view owned by that user.
CREATE PROCEDURE	Enables a user to create a PL/SQL procedure, function or package owned by that user.
CREATE PUBLIC SYNONYM	Enables a user to create a public synonym.
CREATE SEQUENCE	Enables a user to create a sequence owned by that user.
CREATE SESSION	Enables a user to create a connection to the database.
CREATE SYNONYM	Enables a user to create a private synonym.
CREATE TABLE	Enables a user to create a table owned by that user.
CREATE VIEW	Enables a user to create a view owned by that user.
DELETE ANY TABLE	Enables a user to delete from any table in the database.
DROP ANY CACHE GROUP	Enables a user to drop any cache group in the database.
DROP ANY INDEX	Enables a user to drop any index in the database.
DROP ANY	Enables a user to drop any materialized

MATERIALIZED VIEW	view in the database.
DROP ANY PROCEDURE	Enables a user to drop any PL/SQL procedure, function or package in the database.
DROP ANY SEQUENCE	Enables a user to drop any sequence in the database.
DROP ANY SYNONYM	Enables a user to drop a synonym owned by any user in the database.
DROP ANY TABLE	Enables a user to drop any table in the database.
DROP ANY VIEW	Enables a user to drop any view in the database.
DROP PUBLIC SYNONYM	Enables a user to drop a public synonym.
EXECUTE ANY PROCEDURE	Enables a user to execute any PL/SQL procedure, function or package in the database.
INSERT ANY TABLE	Enables a user to insert into any table in the database. It also enables the user to insert into any table using the synonym, public or private, to that table.
LOAD ANY CACHE GROUP	Enables a user to load any cache group in the database.
REFRESH ANY CACHE GROUP	Enables a user to flush any cache group in the database.
SELECT ANY SEQUENCE	Enables a user to select from any sequence or synonym on a sequence in the database.
SELECT ANY TABLE	Enables a user to select from any table, view, materialized view, or synonym in the database.
UPDATE ANY TABLE	Enables a user to update any table or synonym in the database.

---oOo---

Appendix 2 - SYSDBA and SYSOPER Privileges

The following operations are authorized by the SYSDBA and SYSOPER system privileges:

SYSDBA: This system privilege effectively allows a user granted SYSDBA to connect as user SYS.

- STARTUP and SHUTDOWN database operations
- ALTER DATABASE: open, mount, back up, or change character set
- ALTER DATABASE ARCHIVELOG
- ALTER DATABASE RECOVER
- CREATE DATABASE
- CREATE SPFILE
- DROP DATABASE

SYSOPER: This privilege allows a user to perform basic operational tasks, but without the ability to look at user data.

- STARTUP and SHUTDOWN database operations
- ALTER DATABASE OPEN/MOUNT/BACKUP
- ALTER DATABASE ARCHIVELOG
- ALTER DATABASE RECOVER (Complete recovery only.)
- CREATE SPFILE

---oOo---

Appendix 3 - SQL commands which can be disabled

The following SQL*Plus commands can be disabled using the PRODUCT_USER_PROFILE table:

- ALTER
- ANALYZE
- AUDIT
- CONNECT
- COPY
- CREATE
- DELETE
- DROP
- EDIT
- EXECUTE
- EXIT
- GET
- GRANT
- HOST (or the operating system's alias for HOST, such as $ on VMS and ! on UNIX)
- INSERT
- LOCK
- NOAUDIT
- QUIT
- PASSWORD
- RENAME
- REVOKE
- RUN
- SAVE
- SET (see note below)

- SELECT
- SET ROLE
- SET TRANSACTION
- SPOOL
- START
- TRUNCATE
- UPDATE
- You can also disable the following PL/SQL commands:
- BEGIN
- DECLARE

---oOo---

About the author

Malcolm Coxall, the author, is a business and IT systems analyst and consultant with more than 30 years free-lance experience in Europe and the Middle East. Malcolm has worked in Oracle systems design and development for the last 25 years as a developer, business analyst, database designer, DBA, systems administrator, team lead and project manager.

With the experience of working for many of the world's largest corporate and institutional players, as well as for several government and international agencies, Malcolm has extensive hands-on experience in designing and building large-scale Oracle systems in many diverse vertical markets such as banking, oil, defence, telecoms, manufacturing, mining, food, agriculture, aerospace, and engineering.

Malcolm also writes and publishes books, papers and articles on human system design, sociology, environmental economics, sustainable technology and technology in environmental protection and food production.

Apart from his consultancy work, Malcolm's company has designed and built the Oracle Apex cloud systems known as BioTrack and EcoBase. BioTrack is an integrated agriculture and food production control and traceability system designed specifically for organic and other specially controlled food production industries. EcoBase is an environmental research database for bringing together environmental data with complex statistical analysis techniques. Both of these systems were designed and developed in Oracle 10g and are commercialised as cloud-based systems, directly available to end-users.

Malcolm lives in southern Spain from where he continues his free-lance Oracle consultancy and his writing, whilst managing the family's organic farm.

---oOo---